Her Truth

Brittany Mask

PAGE PUBLISHING, INC.
Conneaut Lake, PA

First originally published by Page Publishing 2021

ISBN 978-1-6624-2191-4 (pbk)
ISBN 978-1-6624-2192-1 (digital)

Printed in the United States of America

Summer 1993
Kendall
Eight Years Old

MOST OF THE time Aaron and I would be laughing at people walking down the street or at funny cars we saw, but the car ride was unusually quiet. I was deep in thought, not knowing what to expect when we got to my mother's. Aaron tried a couple of times to cheer me up, but after a light chuckle and no jokes quickly spat back, he decided it was best to leave me be.

"You okay, Doll?" my dad asked, stroking my hair as I watched the scenery pass.

I nodded my head, not changing my position.

"We're going to have a good summer, Kendall," Aaron tried to soothe from the back seat.

I gave a slight smile before saying, "I hope so."

My dad removed his hand and sighed before the car went back to silence.

Aaron had asked his mom and dad if he could go with me to my mother's house for that summer right after the last day of school. His parents agreed because it would not be that far away. They said that it would be good for him to get out of the house and agreed that it would be better for us to play together over the summer. My mother lived in the next town over in Awanaville, Tennessee. I could never say the name of the town correctly. I would always call it Annawannaville. My dad would always shake his head while trying to correct me multiple times before laughing and giving up.

It was two days into Aaron and I starting our summer at my mother's. To my surprise, he and I were having a blast. My mother had a lot of board games, two dogs, and a huge back-yard, so it was not hard for us to find something to do. My mother let us camp in the backyard the night of the second day. We told scary stories and found funny shapes in the stars. Gurdie, my mother's Saint Bernard, would occasionally scare us from barking as we told our scary stories. My mother made us keep her outside with us. "For protection," was what she said. I didn't understand why. There was literally nobody outside after the streetlights came on.

I'm not sure what time Aaron and I went to sleep; however, waking up was more shocking than pleasant. Our tent had been knocked over, and we were being soaked with a water hose.

"What the hell!" Aaron was on his feet, screaming, before I realized what was going on.

When I finally was able to make out the hose and who was holding it, I froze. I could not move. I couldn't even scream, "Stop." He continued to hold the water on me until Aaron pulled me off the ground.

"What's your problem?" he asked.

Aaron pushed me behind him as he stepped up to chal-lenge. Our tormentor laughed as he threw the hose on the ground.

"Just having a little fun."

He walked into the house, taking Gurdie with him. I ran to turn off the hose that was left on.

"Who was that?"

Aaron was picking the tent up.

"My brother. My mom is going to be mad that we're all wet." I picked the sleeping bag up. "And my sleeping bags too?" I sat on the ground, on the brink of tears.

"Why would she be mad at us? It's not our fault. We will just tell her what happened."

My eyes got big as I jumped up.

"No! We can't!" I scrambled to get everything together. "It will be worse. Just let it…"

"Are you two, um, what in the world?" I dropped every-thing as my mother entered the backyard. "Why are you wet?" I looked past my mother and saw my brother standing by the back door. "Kendall, you answer me," she demanded.

"Well, um, um," I started trying to think of a lie.

"You better spit it out."

"It was her brother," Aaron said, coming to stand next to me.

"No," I whispered in his ear.

He continued, "We got woken up by him spraying us with the water hose."

She stood there for a moment, I assume processing her surroundings.

"Levi, get out here!" She did not even turn around to see that he was already standing in the door. It was like she just knew he was there, lurking. He stepped out, never taking his eyes off me. "Did you do this?"

She never looked at Levi as she continued to process the soaked yard and mangled tent. He sucked his teeth.

"Man, I was just playing with them."

Her eyes darted to him, causing her focus to finally detour from the scene.

"Playing? They are soaked!" She pointed at us. I moved a little behind Aaron to avoid Levi's piercing scold then followed my mother's point. "What have I told you about messing with your sister? She is not a ragdoll nor a plaything you can just toss around. You two go dry off. Levi, clean this up, and I mean every bit of it."

We ran inside to my room without saying anything. Aaron got a pair of dry clothes and went to the bathroom that was across the hall from my room. I heard the shower come on and sat in the middle of the floor. I could not hold back the tears. I could only imagine my punishment.

My back was facing the door as I looked through my drawers for a fresh pair of clothes. I felt a pair of eyes watching me, and I assumed it was Aaron because I heard the shower turn off.

I quickly dried my face and asked without turning around, "What do you want to eat? I think my mom has Apple Jacks."

"You know what I want," sounded like a loudspeaker went off in my ears.

I dropped the two shirts that I was holding, quickly closed the drawer, and turned around. Levi was standing in front of my door, which he had closed behind him.

"Levi, please," I begged. "He doesn't know. I promise it won't happen again."

I tried to back up as he moved closer, but I quickly realized that my attempts were in vain. There was nowhere to go. My dresser sat in a nice little nook, in between two walls; it made my room look less cluttered and bigger than it actually was. It also gave Levi the corner that he needed to trap me.

"I know it won't." A grin spread across his face as he unbuckled his pants. "And just to make sure it won't happen again, I want you to taste the consequences." He pulled the front of his pants down, exposing himself. "Literally."

His grin widened into a smile as tears welled up in my eyes again.

I shook my head and pleaded, "Please don't make me do this."

I could still taste the salty flesh from the last time.

"It's only fair, right?" was his response.

Standing straight up, I stood right under his chest; therefore, it took almost nothing for him to be able to push me down to pelvis height. I cried, wishing somebody would walk in before this *thing* entered my mouth. My prayers went unanswered. I gagged as it touched my tongue. The doorknob turned, but the door didn't open. Then there was a knock.

"Ken, why you lock the door?"

Levi pushed me back, causing me to hit my head on the dresser, and quickly fixed his clothes. He laughed as he walked over to the door, putting a finger over his lips, motioning for me to keep quiet. He opened the door and walked past Aaron without saying anything. Aaron stood at the door, confused

"What's going on?" he asked.

Kendall
2015

> *May 15, 2002*
>
> *Dear Lizzie,*
> *Today is the day! Aaron and I are starting our adult lives. That's right! It's graduation day! I cannot wait to see what the rest of life has for us. I know it's going to be hard because we are going to different colleges, but I don't believe that that will change anything...*

I sit in my old room at my father's house, reading an old diary entry. It seems like I wrote this just yesterday. A tear forms in my eye as I think of my old friend.

"What happened to us?" escapes my lips softly.

I close the book and look around the stale room. The Nelly and Justin Timberlake posters hanging on my wall over my desk made me chuckle. Obsessed was not the word for my addiction to these two men. I look at the boxes of sneakers that I have lining the back wall next to my desk and continue to the bedroom door.

"I did not realize that I had so many. I suppose now is a good enough time, if any, to sell them."

I get off the bed and go over to the window in the right corner of the room, still holding my diary. I smile as I remember many mornings and nights writing to Lizzie. When I was younger, my mother had two dogs. Gurdie, my mother's Saint Bernard, was her guard dog. If you were not family or a close family friend, she did not like you. When I was twelve, Gurdie got hit by a car, chasing a cat out of the yard. My mother was devastated. Lizzie, my mother's miniature schnauzer, was my best friend before I even knew what a best friend was. Every time I went to my mom's house, she was right on my heels. We would lay in bed most nights, and I would talk to her. She usually ended up falling asleep while I was talking, but I did not mind. I knew she would keep all my secrets. My mother decided after Gurdie passed that she did not want a dog anymore and gave Lizzie away. She was only five at the time. I remember being sadder that my mom had given her away to somebody that we did not know instead of letting me keep her at my dad's house. I would write in my diary as I talked to Lizzie sometimes. A lot of times it helped me sort out my words. After my mother gave her away, I started writing to her.

I take a deep breath as I look out of the window at all the people coming in and out of my father's house. The fact that I will never be able to talk to my father again, I still can not wrap my head around. I just talked to him last week. The day after I talked to him he collapsed in his driveway because of a brain aneurysm. It was so sudden. I did not believe it until I had to come home to make the arrangements. A faint knock at the door startles me a little, but I do not bother to turn around.

"I'll be down shortly." I clinch the diary to my chest as I hear the door open. I do not change my position by the window. "I said I'll—"

"I heard what you said."

The baritone voice hit me like a ton of bricks crashing into the ocean. Uncontrollable tears stream down my face as I force my body to remain composed. I have not heard that voice in ten years.

"I want to be alone," I hear my mouth say, but in truth, I want to bury my head in his chest and feel his muscles engulf my small frame.

As if he were reading my mind, I feel him spin me around and pull me into a much-needed hug.

"I'm not going anywhere, and you know that."

I rest my head on his chest and cry for what seems like hours.

I finally look up and examine his face. It has changed over the years. It has filled out, and he now has a nicely trimmed goatee. I move up to his hair where shoulder-length braids are now replaced with a low fade. Change definitely comes with age, but there is no mistaking that this is Aaron Phillips. I pull away, wiping my face.

"Still don't know how to follow directions, I see."

I lean on the wall next to the window and give him a once-over. Time has been good to him. I can't help but notice the weight he has picked up. He always had muscles, but the weight has added just the right amount of *umph* to put him in the "God damn" category.

"Still being a mule, I see. How you been?" he spats back.

He sits on my bed, and I notice him giving me the same once-over that I gave him. I turn back to look out of the window.

"Okay for the most part…" I state plainly.

"You cannot still be mad at me."

I remain silent. Honestly, I want us to go back to the way things were between us, like things were when we first met, when being mad at each other was nonexistent.

Fourth Grade, 1994
Aaron
Age Nine

"You know you got a big-ass head. I don't know why you always decide to sit right in front of me."

It was story time in Ms. Robinson's class, and it never failed. Kendall always had to come sit right in front of me so I could not see the pictures.

"Kendall, you know I was going to sit here today," Sasha Anthony said, standing over Kendall.

She did not say anything nor did she move. Everybody in class knew that Sasha liked me, and everybody knew that she did not like Kendall. Sasha probably didn't like Kendall because we always played together on the playground and walked home from school together. I thought it was weird because I did not talk to Sasha at all. She would always bug me, wanting to sit by me at lunch and stand by me in line, but I never wanted to do any of those things.

"Man, Sasha, why don't you just sit beside her? It ain't like you'll be any closer to Aaron," my cousin Tyson Phillips said, causing the class to laugh, but I did not.

Sasha looked around the class, embarrassed, and stomped off to the back of the class. Her pink-and-red barrettes hit the side of her face and you could see the anger in her body.

Kendall looked back at me and rolled her eyes. She and I had an argument when we were walking to school. Kendall told me the next time Sasha came over to her, being mean and trying to tell her what to do, she was going to punch her in the face. I asked her not to because I knew she would be in trouble and get suspended. "Then who would I play with on the playground?" was my closing argument.

Still laughing, Ty nudged me and said, "Man, they are going to fight one of these days, and I can't wait."

"I'm not going to let that happen," I said matter-of-factly.

"I don't know why they fightin' over you."

He laughed harder as I shook my head and turned my attention forward to Ms. Robinson, who was taking her seat.

As we walked after school, Kendall was still upset.

"I don't know why you don't just let me hit the girl."

"Ooh, please do!" Ty happily chimed in as he caught up to us.

"That way she will leave both of us alone," Kendall finished her statement.

"No, because if you do that, who will I talk to?"

I kicked a rock in my path as she answered, "You have Ty."

She giggled after saying it.

"Yeah, man, you will have me," Ty tried to mimic Kendall. I rolled my eyes.

"Y'all coming over? I got the new *Sonic* on SEGA," I asked to change the subject.

"No, I have to go visit my mom today." She looked at the ground as she talked.

"You want me to go with you? I know my mom and dad won't mind."

She did not respond. Our walk home was not long. Ty lived the closest to the school, and we got to his house first.

"If y'all are here tomorrow and come outside, come get me. I don't want to be with Cameron all day."

Kendall and I agreed before continuing our walk.

"Joshua Green was staring at you today when we were in line for lunch," I said to her, trying to pick her mood up.

She had had a crush on Joshua since the beginning of the school year.

A smile creeped on her face, as she looked at me and questioned, "For real?"

I smiled really big and looked straight ahead before yelling, "Nope," as loud as I could.

"Ugh, you play so much," she said, pushing me.

I could not control my laughter.

"You should have seen your face," I said, trying to breathe in between laughing.

"That's why I'm telling Sasha you like her back, and you want her to sit next to you on the bus while we are on our field trip."

I stopped laughing and looked at her, knowing that she was dead serious.

"Come on, don't do that," I said as she held her smile, and we kept walking.

"You never know, you might like the girl. You didn't like me at first, and look at us now."

"No, that's not true. I was the one who came up to you remember? And plus, you don't *like me* like me, and you make me laugh. She is just"—I twisted my face—"yucky!"

Kendall stopped and laughed.

"You couldn't think of a better word?"

I thought about the word I used to describe Sasha, and it seemed very fitting to me.

"Yes, yes, that is the word I want to use."

She laughed so hard it made me laugh.

I never really liked talking to people or making new friends. My mom always said that I was shy, but I honestly did not care to be around anybody. I'd much rather sit back and watch. Kendall was the same, which was how we became friends in the first place. When we met in the second grade, we were in the same class, but she did not really talk to anybody. She would always answer the questions when the teacher asked, but other than that, she would be by herself. One day I saw her down the street from my house, writing on the sidewalk with chalk. I asked my dad if I could go to Ty's house because her house was on the way there. Because Ty and I are cousins, he agreed after telling me to call as soon as I got there. I made a detour by her house, and we've been friends since.

Kendall
2015

"So how's Melanie?" I ask halfheartedly.

I continue to look out the window as more people that I do not know come in and out of the house, some people carrying plates of food. I had not eaten since yesterday morning, so just looking at the plates is making my stomach growl. As if on cue, there is a light knock on the door, and my aunt Lisa's voice follows, as she opens the door.

"Hey, Ken-doll, I thought you might be hungry, so I brought you a plate."

I turn from the window as she notices Aaron sitting on the bed.

"I didn't know you had a guest up here, sorry." She starts to walk back out of the room.

"I haven't grown up that much, have I, Ms. Lisa?"

She turns back, looking a bit confused. She looks at me, and I nod my head, as if I know what she is thinking.

"Aaron?" She smiles wide. "Can't be!" She laughs. "Boy, don't just sit there. Come here and give me a hug." He stands from the bed, and she gives a look of approval. "I see you caught up with yourself. Twenty years younger I might have to snatch you up myself." He hugs her. "*Oh,* and strong too?" They pull back, and she gives him another look of approval. "I ain't seen you since you two were in college. How you been?"

"I'm good, Ms. Lisa. What about you?"

She comes into the room and puts the plate of food on the desk.

"I am blessed, baby. God is good."

"All the time," Aaron agrees as she walks back to the door.

"I'll let you two catch up. Ken, if you need anything, I'll be downstairs."

"Yes, ma'am. Thank you for the food," I say as she leaves the room.

The tension in the room is thicker than a block of government cheese.

"You going to answer my question?"

He takes his place on the bed as I move to the plate of food.

"Cut the bullshit, Kendall. You and I both know you don't give a damn about how Melanie is doing."

I sit at the desk and look at the food. All these years, and this lady is still trying to get me to eat these nasty-ass greens.

"It doesn't hurt to ask."

I turn my attention away from the food and back to Aaron. Looking at the food made me lose my appetite.

We sit in an awkward silence, and I cannot stand it.

"So how have you been? Since you refuse to leave."

He chuckles at my smug comment. I really do not want him here, and he knows that.

"I have a son. He's three. I named him Logan."

I look at him, trying to hold in my laughter but fail. For the first time in what seems like ages, I laugh so hard my stomach begins to hurt.

"I don't know why I'm surprised. Out of all the names in the world, that is what you chose."

He laughs and looks at me as if I should know better than to question his motives.

"Wolverine is only the best comic-book superhero, ever. I could have named him Wolverine."

"Oh god!"

"You got kids?" he asks as our laughter dies down.

"Nope. No kids. No man. Just an old lady and her two cats."

I look back at the food, but my stomach is in knots.

"Just eat the food." I look at him then back at the food. "Well, give it here. I will take the first bite. If it's poisoned, tell my mama I love her."

I laugh a little and move the greens to the far side of the plate. I honestly don't want any of this. I know that the juice from the greens got on everything else on the plate. That completely messed up the baked macaroni and cheese, fried chicken and fish, lasagna and roll.

"The juice is on everything."

I look back at him with my lip poking out. He shakes his head. As children, he knew if greens were on the plate, there is no way I was touching anything else. There have been many times he made me a second plate at cookouts that I couldn't attend because he knew that my dad would always put the "nastiness" on the one he made.

"Just eat the top until you get to the part with the juice."

I roll my eyes at him but take his suggestion.

July 28, 2002
Aaron
Age Eighteen

Kendall and I sat in my dad's 1998 Nissan Altima, waiting on Ty. I was going to pick up Sasha after leaving his house. It was our last night together before we all went our separate ways. We decided that we just wanted it to be us four. We did not know what we wanted to do, but as long as we did it together, we were all happy. Kendall sat in the front passenger seat with the window down. Her head was out of the window; the warm breeze hit her face. She wore her hair in small individual braids that stopped mid-back. As she hung her head out the window, occasionally the breeze would catch the braids and blow them in the wind. The sun setting kissed her walnut skin perfectly. I could not stop staring. The radio played as she looked at me, smiling, dancing to the music.

"I love this song," she said as she turned the volume on the radio up, but it was like a blur in my head.

"Ken, I want to tell you something."

She continued dancing as she questioned, "What's up?" while going back to hanging out the window.

I smiled but turned the music down, causing her to come back in the car.

"What you doing? I was listening to that."

"I saw." I smiled as she rolled her eyes. "I want to tell you something, and I need you to listen."

She huffed as she repositioned herself toward me. I debated if I really wanted to do this. If I did, I could never take it back.

"Kendall, I…"

"Hey, y'all, I want to go too." Ty's brother Camron came to the passenger-side window, scaring both Kendall and me. Kendall pushed his head out of the window, seemingly out of reflex. "Ouch, man, you ain't have to hit me that hard," he screamed as he put his head back in the window.

"You know better than to sneak up on people. And no, you can't come. It's just the four of us," Kendall spoke, adjusting herself in her seat.

Camron sucked his teeth and said, "Come on. I don't want to stay home by myself. My dad is leaving too."

"I know you have some friends you can hang out with. Where is Samantha?" I asked, referring to his girlfriend.

Camron was two years younger than us, and he was every bit of the annoying little brother that I never wanted. Most of the time we would go out my uncle Trevor, their dad, would make us take him with us. Throughout the years it wasn't that bad, tagging him along, but this time was a no go.

"She got grounded yesterday, and Miguel just left for Florida."

He pouted as he referred to his best friend.

"Cam, you not going," Ty said as he got in the back seat behind Kendall.

"Dad told me if Aaron said I could, then I can go."

Both Kendall and Ty looked at me, waiting on me to say no. I shook my head.

"Sorry, man. When we all come back in town, you are on the VIP list to hang out with us."

He sucked his teeth before moving away from the car.

"That's okay. Y'all are going to need me one day, and I'ma be like, remember that time y'all left me."

Kendall smirked and said, "Aw Cam, don't be like that. You know we love you."

"Man, whatever."

He turned to go back into the house, and I pulled off.

"Do we know what we are doing yet?" Ty asked as he leaned on the center console.

"Naw. Figured we would figure it out when Sash got in the car. Maybe we can go to the park and just chill. I don't want to do anything too fancy. Just hang with my peeps," Kendall closed her eyes as she talked. It looked as though she was soaking in every moment.

"That doesn't sound like a bad idea," I agreed. "Let's see what Sasha says."

Ty finally sat back in the seat as he agreed with the plan as well.

"Y'all scared?" he asked after a second of silence.

"Shitless," I answered honestly, causing us to laugh.

"I don't think it's going to be that bad," Kendall disagreed. "Anything is better than here. I'm ready."

I glanced at her, and she had not changed her position. I looked at Ty through the rearview mirror. He was staring at her in a weird way, like he wanted to say something but couldn't get it out. He noticed me looking at him and quickly looked out the window, not acknowledging that he was caught.

"What about you, Ty?" she questioned.

"Well, not too much is going to change for me. I just won't have y'all here to get on my nerves."

Uncle Trevor was the town's maintenance man. There was not anything he could not fix. My dad always said that it was a gift that skipped over him. "You got to be good with your hands. The only thing my hands are good for is loving," he would joke. Uncle Trevor followed in the footsteps of his father, and Ty was following suit. Even though he got a few scholarships offered, he did not feel that college was for him. He knew he wanted to take up the family business and knew that experience was the only schooling he needed.

Kendall turned in her seat and rebutted, "What you talking 'bout, getting on your nerves? You are going to be bored out of your mind without us. Mark my words."

He shook his head and countered, "Both of y'all will be an hour away in opposite directions. If I get to bored, I will just pop up." He smiled cunningly. "Might even sit in on a class or two."

She rolled her eyes as she turned back in her seat, saying, "I hope they kick you off campus and make you pay some sort of fine or something."

I laughed, "Dang, all that?" I shook my head in disbelief and stated, "That's okay. You're welcome at my school anytime."

"Thank you, Aaron. It's nice to know that somebody cares," he mocked, poking Kendall in the back of the head.

She swatted at his hand, but he was too quick.

"Keep on. I'ma kick yo ass when we get out."

He laughed and joked, "You ain't never been able to kick my ass, and tonight is not about to be the night you will."

"Bet," she said and folded her arms across her chest.

"Bet," he said, poking her in the head again.

I laughed as I pulled up to Sasha's apartment building. We had all gotten new cell phones as a graduation present from our parents, and we were all too excited.

We all had unlimited text and free nights and weekends. We thought we were big stuff. I texted Sasha, letting her know that we were downstairs.

"Kendall, can you run up and let Sasha know we are here," I asked as I put my phone back in the pocket that I had taken it out of to send the text.

"Didn't you just text her?" she asked, clearly annoyed.

"Yeah, but you know how she is, and you know she takes all day."

She softened up, realizing that I was right.

"Yeah, you're right. I'll be back with Sasha in tow."

She got out the car and stretched before making her way toward Sasha's apartment. Once she was out of view, I turned my attention to Ty.

"You got a thing for Kendall?"

I tried not to sound too aggressive. He looked at me, baffled.

"What?" he questioned back, as if I had offended him.

"I saw how you were looking at her a second ago."

He attempted to laugh it off.

"Naw, man, I just think it's weird how bad she's ready to leave here. You don't think that's strange?"

I shook my head.

"No. You are the only strange one. You want to stay."

He gave a genuine laugh and said, "Ain't nothing out there for me but trouble."

"Sounds like a mixture of Uncle Trevor and fear. How you know what's out there if you don't go?" He shook his head as he looked out the window. "This town is my home. If we all move away, who is going to take care of it? My dad isn't that old now, but when he gets to where he can't do anything, who is going to take over? Cam damn sure isn't. He'd rather be out, singing in some girl's ear or playing the guitar than fixing things. Naw, man. This town. This business. This is where I belong."

"I wholeheartedly disagree. The company is going to be here when you get back. The experience that you will get just going away for a little while will be a lifetime of memories and new friendships. Just think about it at least. Take this semester, maybe even the year, but don't completely shut it down."

He nodded, more than likely just to shut me up.

"I'll think about it. But I don't have a thing for Kendall." He went back to my original question. "Everybody knows that is your girl." I returned his initial baffled look as if I had no idea what he was talking about. "Man, don't come at me with that bullshit. You and Kendall are made for each other."

I turned back in my seat and exhaled.

"I don't know about that one."

Ninth Grade
Kendall
Age Fourteen

I stood beside my locker, waiting on Aaron when I heard my name being called. I did not bother to answer because I already knew who it was. I had been avoiding her all week. I found over the years that, that was the best way to get rid of her. This time, unfortunately, it was not going to work. For whatever reason, our biology teacher, Mr. Crenshaw, decided that it would be a brilliant idea to make Sasha and I partners for our class project. All the years I had been avoiding being in the same area as her, and here he came, wanting us to actually work together. He said, "You two can learn something from each other." I rolled my eyes at the thought of his words. She finally reached me, and I was more annoyed than the first time she called my name.

"You do know we actually have to talk to get this done."

I finally turned my attention to her. Sasha and I were about the same height, and she was a shade darker than me. She still looked the same from the fourth grade, with her almond-shaped eyes and slender lips. The only difference was her hair. It would always be half up in a ponytail and half down with ring curls. She was never a bad-looking girl, just a bad attitude.

"I can't talk to you today. Aaron and I have to go."

I used Aaron as a scapegoat, as I often did to get out of things that I did not want to do. He and I laughed when I found out that he did the same thing.

"Aaron is at basketball practice. I saw him in the gym when I passed by it. So you have at least an hour."

She had her hand on her hip the whole time she was talking and popping her neck.

I rolled my eyes and mentally kicked myself in the ass for forgetting that he had practice.

"I can just do it myself and give you the information when it's done," I said as I turned to open my locker. "It's an easy A, and we don't have to be around each other. It's a win-win."

I opened my locker, blocking her from my view. She took a deep breath and moved to the other side of the locker so that she could see me.

"Forgive me for not wanting to put my 3.8 GPA solely in your hands, but I do not let anyone do my work for me." She leaned back on the lockers as she kept talking. "We don't like each other, and that is fine, but if I get anything less than an A on this, my mom is going to kill me. So I say let's push the dislike aside until we are done, and then we can go back to ignoring and hating each other."

She said it as if she had been rehearsing it for days. I was a little taken aback and impressed. I was not aware that she was as into her grades and GPA as I was. I closed my locker and looked at her.

"Fine, let's go to the library." I instantly regretted it as soon as the words left my mouth.

Without saying another word, she pushed herself off the lockers and started walking in the direction of the library. I followed behind her while putting my math and biology book in my backpack.

We finally got to our destination and picked a table. She did not say anything as she removed her book and three-ring binder from her backpack. She sat and stared at the binder a couple of minutes without saying anything. Although her and I were not friends, it was very apparent that something was bothering her. As she stared at her belongings, I stared at her. It might have seemed very weird, but she was acting strange. It was almost uncomfortable.

"Um, so are we going to do this or no?" I asked, starting to get frustrated. She did not answer. I shook my head and started to pick up my backpack that I had sat on the floor beside my chair. "I knew this wasn't going to work."

"Why are we not friends?" her whispered voice asked.

It was so low I almost missed the question. Caught off guard, I sat my bag back down and looked at her as if she had three heads. Is she serious? I looked around to make sure she was not trying to be funny or play a joke.

"I'm sorry, what?" I finally asked.

"Why are we not friends?" she repeated her question, this time louder, still focused on her binder. I squinted my eyes at her. I could not determine if she was being serious. She looked up from the binder, finally at my face. My look of confusion, shock, and intrigue caused her to fall into laughter. I chuckled as I fixed my face.

"You're serious."

The realization set in as my back fell into the chair. She stopped laughing, and the same uneasy look resurfaced on her face.

For the first time in years, I realized that this was not the attention-seeking, loud, bossy, annoying girl from the fourth grade. The fourteen-year-old girl that I watched grow with me seemed very unsure, almost reclusive. I had only seen her talk to a handful of people and not for long.

"Do you have any friends?" I asked honestly. The how-dare-you look on her face informed me that I had offended her. But that was no cause to back down. "It's a simple question, yes or no."

"You can't answer a question with a question, Kendall."

Her matter-of-fact tone humored me. I sat up, looking at her with the same squinty face as before. We stared at one another, challenging the other with our eyes.

"Because you're a bitch," I answered her question without breaking eye contact.

A smirk creeped on her face, and I fought to hold mine back. My attempt was in vain as laughter filled the space. We laughed so hard we caught the attention of the librarian.

"If you two keep this up, I will have to ask you to leave."

Her abrupt entrance startled us.

"We're sorry. We will keep it down," Sasha said, trying not to laugh.

I put my hand over my mouth, trying to muffle my laughter. The librarian nodded her head at us before leaving. We laughed a little longer before Sasha got serious again.

"You really think I'm a bitch?"

I shook my head in disbelief and stated, "You cannot be serious with these questions. Have you met you?"

She sighed and sat back in her chair, saying, "My mom tells me all the time that I need to watch my tone and the way I talk to people. She says that—"

"Okay, cut the bullshit, Sasha." At this point, I felt like this was some kind of setup. "What happened to 'we don't like each other, and that's fine'? I'm confused right now. Are we not supposed to be working on this project?" She sat there, blankly looking at nothing. "Why are you acting weird? Did Aaron put you up to this? Because this is not funny at all."

"No, Kendall. My question was honest. I know that sometimes I can come off as being abrasive, harsh, a bitch." She mimicked my name-calling. "But I really want to know why we don't get along. From what I've seen over the years, you're as big a bitch as I am."

I laughed a little before saying, "We are nothing alike, Sasha."

"That isn't what Aaron says."

My demeanor changed from intrigue to anger. As far as I knew, Aaron never talked to her. He avoided her as much as I did.

"So you and him are like besties now? Trading secrets and shit. You braid each other's hair too?"

She chuckled at my aggression. I could see that my anger was entertaining her.

"You know, Kendall, if you got your head out of Aaron's ass every once in a while, you would see that you are not the only person in his life."

I could not hold back any longer. Before I knew what my body was doing, I felt the impact of my fist hitting her face. Promptly after her biology book was on the side of my head, knocking me out of my chair. I stumbled up to launch at her, but I could not reach her. I looked down at my waist to a pair of arms holding me back.

"Sasha, go before you get suspended," I heard his voice in my ear.

"Tyson, let me go," I hollered.

"Man, shut up," he harshly whispered in my ear. "Get your shit and let's go."

As he was talking, the librarian came around the corner, "Is there a problem?" She asked.

"No, ma'am, we were just leaving," Ty answered back, letting me go.

She nodded her head, and I picked up my backpack. We walked out of the library with him guiding me.

"Have you lost your mind?"

He was clearly upset, but I did not care. I quickly glanced around the empty hallway in front of the library door, looking for Sasha. I had been waiting for this moment for five years. I was not going to let Tyson take that from me. "Kendall, are you listening to me?" I did not respond. He sucked his teeth. "Come on, man, you know this is not how you want your freshman year to go. Chill out." I still did not say anything. "Think about it. You get suspended, your mom and dad are pissed, and you have to stay home with your brother."

That caught my attention and caused me to calm down a little.

"Where is Aaron?" I asked because him being here meant that practice was over.

"His dad was waiting on him after practice. You weren't there, so I guess they thought you left." I sucked my teeth, knowing that I had to walk home. "I'm walking if you want to walk with me. I just have to get a book from the library."

I nodded and followed him back into the library.

"So you and Sasha?" Ty started as we walked out of the school.

He had gotten his book, and we were starting our trek home. I had calmed down a little while waiting on him to find the book that he needed.

"What about us?" I looked at him, waiting on his reply.

"Please don't hit her," he said, looking straight ahead. I looked in the direction that he was looking and got mad all over again. I started taking my backpack off as he stepped in front of me. "Kendall. Please do not fight her."

"The bitch hit me in the face with a book."

I could tell that he was trying not to laugh as he held me back.

Sasha reached us and proclaimed, "I am not here to fight you."

"Well, she really wants to fight you" Ty rebutted, still holding me back.

She sighed and continued, "I want to apologize. I should not have let things get that out of hand. I honestly want us to be friends."

Two weeks had gone by, and Sasha and I had managed to get most of our project done without incident. We met after school for an hour each day. When it got closer to the time to turn the project in, we would go to each other's house to try and finish. During those times, we got very little done because we ended up laughing and talking about things completely unrelated to biology. Boys were mostly the main topic. Sasha was the oldest of three siblings and lived with her mother who was single and trying to make ends meet. Going to Sasha's house became freeing for me. I would help her cook and play with her sister and brother and not have to worry about somebody lurking behind me. Staying at my house was a different story when Levi was around. I always did my very best to make sure that she was never in a room alone with him.

"Your brother is weird," she plainly stated the first night she was able to sleep over my dad's house.

It was a month after we had turned in our project, and we were almost inseparable. Her mom and my parents finally met and agreed that it was great that we were hanging out together.

"About time you have a girl to hang out with," my mom said after their meeting.

"Yeah, just try to avoid him when he's here." I tried my best not to give off any weird vibes when talking about him.

"What is it like going back and forth from your dad to your mom's?"

I sat on my window seat, writing to Lizzie, and she talked and asked her questions from my bed.

"It's not that bad. I prefer to stay here at my dad's. My brother and I don't really get along, so I try to be where he is not."

"Do you feel like an only child sometimes?"

I stopped writing as I thought about her question. My brother had always been around in some form or fashion, so I never thought of my time away from him as being an only child, but I guess sometimes I was.

"I guess sometimes I do. I mean, of course, I know I still have a brother, but it's nice to not have him around all the time," I spoke before thinking. "Oh, I'm sorry."

She laughed and stated, "No need to be sorry. My brother and sister are a handful, but I wouldn't trade them for the world."

"That must be nice," I somberly said, causing her to chuckle as if it was a joke.

"Hey, what ya writing?"

She started to get off the bed, moving closer to me. I closed the book and set it to the side. She nodded her head, as if understanding that it was personal.

"Hey, you want to see what I drew today?" she asked.

"Of course, I do!"

I was excited. She was one of the best artists I had ever met in person. I was a little jealous because I could barely draw a circle. She went in her overnight bag and pulled out her sketchbook. She flipped a few pages then handed it to me. I was in awe. She had drawn the top three basketball players in our school on their own basketball cards. It almost looked as though they were real NBA player cards. In total, there were six cards. Each one had a front and back with their updated stats.

"I'm going to take it to the school newspaper on Monday to see if they want to use it," she said, unsure. "You think they will like it?"

I scrunch up my face and declared, "Anybody who says they don't like it, you point them my way. This is amazing."

She blushed, saying, "Thank you."

"You stop it! You know these are bomb." I handed her back her sketchbook. "You ever thought about what you want to do when you graduate?" I asked her as she put her book back in her bag.

"Not really. I want to draw, but my mom says there aren't any good paying jobs in that. She wants me to be like a doctor or something. Who wants to stay in school that long?"

I laughed and said, "I think I'm going to go to the newspaper with you on Monday. I have a couple of articles they might like."

"You write? Can I see something?"

I was a little hesitant before going into my backpack and pulling out a thick binder full of different articles that I thought would be interesting, along with snippets of photos that I thought the page should look like. I cringed as I handed it to her.

"Don't judge me too hard."

I twirled a random piece of my hair as I watched her flip through the pages with a smile plastered on her face. An occasional "oh my god!" or "Kendall!" was yelled throughout the turning of the pages.

"If this was a magazine, I would subscribe like yesterday. This is so good."

"You think so?" I asked shyly.

"Girl, yes. Who else has seen this?"

I shrugged and replied plainly, "Aaron."

"Oh no, ma'am. You are most definitely coming with me on Monday." I smiled as she handed the binder back to me then snatched it back again. "Wait, I want to look at it again."

Aaron
2015

"Ty told me he saw you last week."

Watching her pick over her food has always been frustrating. We both know that she is not going to eat it, so I do not understand why she does not just take it back.

"We had lunch on Monday. It was nice. He promised that we wouldn't talk about you."

I nervously rub my head. "Oh" is all I can get out. Growing up, I never would have guessed that she and I would be where we are now. Throughout the years, I've tried to reach out to her and tried to rekindle our friendship. All to no avail.

"Well, I'm glad you still keep in touch with somebody."

She looks at me, confused.

"What are you talking about? I talk to Sasha almost every day," she says.

"That's 'cause her ass still ain't got no friends." She shakes her head. "She's actually married with two kids." "I know. We're friends on Shadow." I refer to a social-media site where everybody that we went to high school with has a group page, and everybody tells how "exciting" their life is right now. "She sends me a message every now and then."

She nods her head.

"Do you want me to fix you another plate? You are clearly not going to eat that," I say.

I have grown tired of watching her pick over her plate. She puts the plate on the desk and gets up. I watch her every move. I can tell that she has let her ear-length hair grow out even though it is currently in a neat bun on the top of her head. The little makeup that she had on has gotten messed up from her crying, but that has not taken anything from her beauty. She still looks the same as I last saw her. Her mature face has finally caught up with her doe eyes, but it looks as though she has maintained her 150-pound weight. She looks as though life has been good to her.

She moves back toward the window.

"I'm going back down in a little while," she says, sitting on the window seat, watching people from the window. She takes a quick look at her diary, picks it up, and smiles.

"I'm sorry," I say, not knowing how she is going to respond.

"Can we not do this right now?" she says as she looks back out the window.

"If not now, when?" I get agitated. "It's not like you answer any of my calls. You get mad if Ty or Sasha even mentions my name. If you see me in public, you avoid me at all cost. Yes, I've seen you in the mall several times. The only reason I know you don't live in town anymore is because Ty told me. I cannot keep doing this, Kendall!" I get off the bed and move toward her. "I want my best friend back." She does not move. If Kendall is nothing else, she is stubborn, always has been. It has always driven me up a wall.

"How's Melanie?" she asks, still not diverting from the window. "Does she even know you're here?"

I do not answer. The truth is, she does not know that I am here. This was supposed to be a quick hi-and-bye. I was going to come and pay my respects to Mr. Lancaster and go back home. Seeing Kendall, knowing how close she was with her father and how much pain she is most likely in right now, I could not bear to leave her alone. Not this time, not again.

"Does that matter right now?" I ask.

I can feel her piercing stare, even though I am looking right at her. The moment she turned to face me seemed like she snapped her neck. In fact, I think I heard a pop.

"What the hell kind of question is that? You know what, I need you to leave!" She gets up from her seated position and moves toward me, tossing her diary on the bed. "Right now. I want you out of my daddy's house! You are no longer welcome here!" she yells and pushes me toward the door.

"Kendall, we have to deal with this at some point." I dodge her pushes and move around to the other side of her.

"Get out!" she yells, doubling back toward me.

There is a knock at the door, causing us to stop in our tracks. I take my place back on the bed in an attempt to stand my ground. I am not leaving until we resolve this and at least be cordial. The door opens and her mother sticks her head in the door.

"Kendall, is everything okay?" she asks as she scans the room.

Her eyes settle on me as I stand to greet her.

"Oh no, sir. Do not come over here, trying to hug me," she says as she makes her way in the room, closing the door behind her. "No. You are not allowed to speak to me until you two stop this foolishness."

She folds her arms across her chest as her eyes dart back and forth from Kendall to me.

"That's what I'm trying to do, Ms. Cynthia, but you know your daughter."

Sophomore year, Christmas Break 2003
Kendall
Age Nineteen

I was so excited to be going home. Both Aaron and Sasha said that they were going to be home too. Three weeks before our break, my dad told me that my brother had got put in jail. For me it was a Christmas miracle. I could spend Christmas with my family and friends drama-free. We all decided to spend Christmas morning with our families, but as soon as we were done, everybody would meet at my dad's house, just like in high school.

The day I got home my dad told me that we would be spending Christmas at my mom's. He said that it was because he did not want to cook and get his kitchen dirty, but I thought otherwise. I would see the way my dad acted toward my mother and listen to the way he talked about her. I could tell that after all the years of them not being together, he was still in love with her. I wondered how different things would have turned out if they would have stayed together. I wondered if Levi would have treated me the way that he did.

Christmas morning Aunt Lisa, my dad's sister, showed up at my dad's house at six in the morning. I had already antici-pated her arrival the night before and made sure that my door was locked. I loved her to pieces, but she could be a bit much, especially when you were trying to catch up on the sleep you lost during the semester. The locking of my door was no deterrent for her as she banged on the door until I let her in the room.

"This is the day that the Lord was born. We shall rejoice and be glad in it."

She hugged me as soon as the door opened.

"That is not how that goes, Aunt Lisa."

I rested my tired body on her as I talked. She pulled away.

33

"I know you ain't still sleep." She turned me around into my room. "Come on now. We have things to do and places to be. And I got you an extra special present this year."

I chuckled as she pushed me to my closet.

"You say that every year, Auntie."

"So! My gifts are always amazing. Say I'm wrong."

She stopped pushing me and sat at my desk, waiting for me to pick my outfit for the day. She was not leaving the room until she knew that I was not going to get back in the bed.

"I mean it was that one time," I joked.

"You can't be talking about that time we all agreed not to talk about." I shrug. "Hey, lady, you woke me up out of a great sleep. I say things of truth in this state."

I had piqued her interest as I rummaged through my duffle bag to find the outfit that I had pre-picked for Christmas day.

"Is that a fact?" Her tone was mischievous. "What do you think about your mother's new man, Jerry?"

I looked back at her and her devilish smile, laughing as I turned back to my bag.

"I met him the last time I was home. He's a little too quiet if you ask me. Seems sneaky."

"Right!" She emphatically agreed. "Your uncle and I went on a double date with them a couple of weeks ago, and it was very uncomfortable. He sat there, eating bread and chuckling. Every now and then he would throw in a 'I know what you mean.' It was weird." I laughed as she told her story. "Dante, they broke up last week? Something about he just stopped calling?" I questioned as I continued to rummage. "Like I say he was a weird one. What about you? You seeing any of them nice college mens?"

I knew the question was going to come up at some point in my visit, and I answered with my prepared answer.

"I'm just focused on school. I barely notice any of the guys there."

"Barely, you say."

I shook my head, and I pulled my white sweater and dark denim jeans out my bag.

"I'm about to get ready now," I said as I turned to put my clothes on my bed.

She sucked her teeth.

"Well," she got out of the chair as she spoke, "Aaron isn't there, so you need to explore your options while you can."

"What does Aaron have to do with anything?" I turned to ask, but she was already out the door.

My mother was always very big when it came to Christmas. Her house was like walking into a Christmas shop every year. That year was surprisingly very minimal decorations. It was more elegant than gaudy. Her tree was decorated with simple red-and-white ornaments draped over her faux snow Christmas tree. The rest of the house had strategically placed red, white, and silver holiday-inspired knickknacks. I was impressed.

"Wow, Ma, this is nice," I complimented as I entered the house behind my dad, aunt, and uncle.

"I thought I would do something a little different this year."

"In other words, her decorations got too old to put out." Aunt Lisa laughed as she took off her coat.

They made me carry all the gifts in as if I was still a child in grade school.

"So y'all just not going to help me with the gifts?" I asked, putting them down beside the tree that was not far from the front door in the living room.

"We already have our coats off. Plus, you young," my dad said as he settled into a chair in the far corner of the room.

I rolled my eyes as I went back to the car for the remaining gifts. As I struggled to close the trunk of my dad's 2000 Saturn, I heard a car pulling up behind me.

"Let me help you with some of those," I heard Aaron's voice coming up behind me.

"Oh my god, Aaron," I squealed before dropping all the presents that I was holding. I threw my arms around his neck as I hugged him tightly. "I thought I wasn't going to see you until later."

I pulled back as he smiled his million-dollar smile.

"I wanted to surprise you."

"Well, color me surprised, punk."

I punched him in the chest. He moved back a little as he laughed.

"I bought somebody for you to meet."

He smiled wider as a girl about an inch or two shorter than me walked up to him. My wide smile turned down a bit as she reached out her hand.

"I'm Melanie. It's Kenda, right?"

I looked at Aaron, slightly offended, but kept my smile as I corrected while shaking her hand.

"Kendall. It's nice to finally meet you, Melanie. I've heard a lot about you."

"I imagine so," she said, letting go of my hand.

My smile faded as I looked at Aaron once again.

"Hey, Kendall, let me help you with these presents so we can get out of this cold weather." I bent down to pick up the gifts that I had dropped, and Aaron did so as well.

"You better get your girl before I do," I whispered harshly.

"She's an acquired taste. Be nice please."

"She gone be real acquired in a minute." We got everything off the ground, and I closed the truck.

"About time. It's freezing," she murmured under her breath, but loud enough for me to hear.

They walked ahead as I attempted to keep my composure. A mixture of anger and disappointment briefly took over, but I quickly shook it off as I entered the house.

"Look who I ran into outside," I announced, trying to hold back the tears that were starting to form.

"Aaron," my dad hollered in excitement, and he jumped up from his seat. "Finally, somebody to talk to about sports. Old Joe D don't know a ball from a stick in the mud."

He joked about my uncle who had taken his place the chair adjacent from my dad.

"Naw, you just mad 'cause the Bulls are garbage. I mean trash."

Aaron laughed as he gave my dad a hug with his empty arm. I sat what I was holding down and quietly excused myself into the half bathroom that was next to the kitchen. As soon as I closed the door, the tears streamed down my face. I could not keep myself together. So many years I had seem Aaron with so many different females, but I could not understand why I was letting Melanie get under my skin. I was not able to stew long. My mother knocked on the door about three minutes later.

"Kendall, come help me get the food started."

I took a deep breath before answering, "Be out in a second." I looked at myself in the mirror. "Get yourself together," I whispered before wiping my tears.

I took a deep breath before leaving the room. I join Aunt Lisa and my mother in the kitchen.

"Start pickin' the peas."

My mother pointed to the plastic grocery bag full of string beans. I sighed as I turned on the sink to fill a bowl with water.

"Is there anything I can do?" her voice entered the kitchen. As my back was turned from the kitchen entrance, I rolled my eyes. "As much as I like talking sports and cars, I think I would do better in here."

I turned to get another grocery back out of the bag drawer and notice Aunt Lisa glancing at me. She shot me a slight smile, and I gave a weak one back.

"Well, what can you cook?" my mother asked as she stirred a pot of spaghetti sauce on the stove.

"Pretty much anything. I love to cook."

I rolled my eyes again as I got my bowel of water out of the sink.

"Okay, well, it's a bag of greens over by the sink. If you can start picking them, that would be great."

I got everything that I needed and moved to the breakfast table, sitting off to the corner of the kitchen. Just because I had to help cook did not mean that I had to socialize. I sat, picking the peas for a moment before hearing my name being whispered. I looked up to see Aaron motioning for me to follow him back to my old room that my mother had turned into a home office. I reluctantly obliged. Before leaving, I noticed my mother and Melanie talking and laughing. I sighed before walking the short distance to the room. As soon as I entered, he closed the door.

"Can you at least pretend to be nice," he hissed.

I folded my arms across my chest as I leaned on the large desk that had replaced my bed.

"Me being silent is me being nice," I stated.

"Ken, come on, man. I really want you two to get along."

"Did you tell her that before she came here with her snippy-ass comments? And who the hell is Kenda? I'm pretty sure the heffa knows my damn name. You want me to be nice to somebody who approached me super disrespectful? You know me better than that, Aaron."

He walked up to me, putting his hands on the elbows of my folded arms.

"You're right. I do. But I also know that you want me to be happy, and she makes me happy."

I sucked my teeth as he pulled me into a hug. He started to squeeze.

"Ouch! Let me go."

I tried to push away. I could feel him laughing.

"Nope. Not until you agree to be nice." He squeezed tighter.

"Nice Kendall? I don't know who she is." I joked as I pushed, causing him to squeeze tighter. "Okay, okay, punk. I'll be nice. Now let me go."

"You pinky dog promise?"

I laughed, remembering our made-up pinky promise.

"Pinky dog! Now let go!" He finally let go, and I pushed him in the chest. "Punk."

He smiled as he folded his arms then asked, "We haven't talked in a couple of weeks. How are you?"

I leaned back on the desk and answered, "I'm okay. Classes were kicking my butt, but I managed to get it together."

"There was no doubt that you wouldn't."

He smiled. There was a silence as we stared at each other.

"Aaron, I…"

"Aaron your parents are here," said my mother as she came in the room without knocking.

"Okay, we'll be right out," he answered without taking his eyes off me. My mother looked at both of us, confused, before leaving. "You were saying?" he said, not missing a beat as the door closed.

I smiled as I pushed myself off the desk.

"I miss you."

I walked past him out of the room, feeling worse than I did when we went in.

The food was done a little after noon. We ate opened gifts then left my mother's house. As planned, Sasha, Ty, Camron, Aaron, and Melanie piled in my dad's living room.

"Kendall, call me if you need me. I'm going to Alvin's Pub," my dad announced as he was walking out the door.

I got off my spot on the floor to give him a hug.

"No, Daddy, *you* call me if *you* need *me*. Don't be out here trying to drive all drunk and whatnot."

He laughed his hardy laugh and said, "Girl, I'm grown." He hugged back.

"Yeah, okay. Be safe, Daddy."

He left, and I took my place back on the floor in between Camron and Sasha who sat on the couch.

"Finally!" Ty stood up. "Cam, come help me right quick."

I looked at Ty, confused.

"Where you going?" Sasha asked, matching my expression.

He sucked his teeth and said, "We'll be right back."

He and Camron walked out the front door, and I took Cam's seat on the couch.

"So, Melanie, right?" Sasha broke the then-awkward silence.

"Yeah," Melanie nodded.

Sasha said as Melanie nodded as she laughed and stated, "It's nice to finally put a face to the name. Aaron hasn't shut up about you since you two met." Melanie laughed. "I can say the same for all of you." Her and Sasha shared a laugh as I looked on, unamused. Aaron cleared his throat and I gave a fake laugh. "Yeah, he never shuts up," I said, causing Sasha to nudge me. "Come on now, Kendall, be nice." "I have been being as nice as I can be," I stated plainly. "Kendall, I owe you an apology." I look at her, both confused and suspicious. "I was very rude this morning, and I should not have been. Aaron wanted so bad for us to meet and hit it off, but I feel like I ruined that right off the bat." I looked at Sasha who was looking back at me.

"I appreciate the apology."

I smiled, but I was not believing a single piece of that apology. I looked at Aaron who had his goofy smile plastered on his face—happy that it seemed like Melanie and I would get along. I chuckled and decided that I would put up with her for his happiness. Seeing him happy made everything else disappear.

"Kendall, can I talk to you. In the kitchen," Sasha said, getting up. "Now please," she demanded.

I sighed before getting up.

"You are not my mother, Sasha," I said, following her out the room.

I did not get in the kitchen good before she started talking.

"Why are you letting this hippie fondle all over him? And what is that silly-ass grin that he has had cemented on his face since he walked in? And I'm not going to even start on that fake-ass apology."

I sighed a breath of relief that somebody else was as upset as I was.

"Sasha, I have been trying my best to be on my best behavior all day."

"I don't know why. She clearly hasn't. She has been all over him since they walked in. She act like we going to kidnap the boy." I chuckled at her dismay as she moved around the kitchen. "Seriously, Kendall. Go tell him how you feel about him and get her out of here."

My chuckle turned in to a blank stare.

"What?"

She focused on me and looked at me as if I had a dragon tail.

"How you feel about him is so obvious, and I wish you would stop pretending like it's not."

"I don't feel—"

"So now we're lying to each other?" She leaned her arms on the counter as she cut me off.

"Sasha, I want him to be happy, and he seems like she is making him the happiest I have ever seen him. The only other time I saw that silly-ass grin was when you and him were together. He was so happy with you. And the fact that we were all friends made it even better. I've been watching him with her all day. Even though I don't care for her, at all, he is obviously walking on air. I will not be the cause of his unhappiness."

She shook her head as she started to leave the room.

"All I know is that you only get one Aaron in your life. He is an amazing guy, and he's yours. All you have to do is speak up."

She left the room, and Ty came in, handing me a Bud Light.

"Beer?" he asked. I turned up my nose. "It's a bottle of gin in the living room. I just came in here to get some cups. Figured you could use something to take the edge off."

I laughed a little.

"What do you think about her?" I asked as I opened the can.

"Well." He sat a couple of cups on the counter then turned back to the cabinet. "She ain't what I thought he would end up with, but he looks happy."

I took a sip of the drink and turned up my nose again.

"That didn't answer my question at all."

He smiled at me and asked, "Can you help me with the cups?"

Eighth Grade, 1998
Aaron
Age Thirteen

The gym door opened, and I saw Kendall walk in with her head down. I wanted to go over to her to see what was wrong, but I knew that that would be extra laps for the team. I watched as she moved to the left bleachers, stomped to the middle, and sat down. She did not even look at the court.

"Mr. Phillips, is there a problem?" Coach Peterman screamed from across the court.

"Come on, man, you know she will still be right there when practice is over," Melvin said as he ran past me down the court.

"No, Coach, I'm good," I yelled back as I ran to my position.

I had been playing the shooting-guard position since the sixth grade. Coach said I'm pretty good at it but wanted to switch me to power forward. He said that because I was getting taller, I would be better at blocking by the goal. I personally did not think that I would be able to do it, but if the coach said I could, I would try it out.

We finished practice, and Kendall was still sitting in the same spot, doing her homework. I ran into the locker room to grab my things.

"What's going on with your girl?" Bobby Sherry asked as he grabbed his things from his locker.

He was about two feet taller than me and looked to weigh maybe eighty more pounds than me. He played center. Rightfully so because he was the tallest person on the team.

"I have no idea. She probably got for an A minus or some-thing. You know how she gets."

He laughed as he closed his locker.

"You know if she is going to the dance with anybody?" he asked, rubbing his freshly cut head.

I laughed a little.

"I don't know, man, you have to ask her."

I grabbed my backpack and threw it over one shoulder.

"I'm asking you. I ain't trying to get played in front of everybody. You saw how she dissed Ronnie Shoubalt."

"Come on now. You really think Kendall would go to the dance with dusty-ass Ronnie?" I asked, and we both laughed.

"I felt sorry for Ron. Man, the look on her face when he walked up to her should have stopped him in his tracks," he said, still laughing. "But for real, you think she'll go with me?"

I shake my head in annoyance.

"Man, I am not Kendall's keeper. You have to ask her yourself." I started to walk off. "But you should probably ask her tomorrow. No telling how long she is going to be in this mood."

He nodded his head, and we gave each other five before I left the locker room.

Some of the guys stayed back after practice and showered. I never liked public showers, and I liked the way the wind felt when I would walk home. It cooled me down. Some days it got so hot a shower would not matter anyway. That day was one of those days. Our walk home started off silent, but it was not for my lack of trying.

"Hey, what's wrong?" I asked, walking backward in front of her.

"I am fine, Aaron, please leave me alone."

She stared past me with a blank yet determined face. It was very unusual for Kendall not to say anything. Typically, if something was bothering her, she had to vent to get it all out. She said it always made her feel better to get whatever it is off her chest.

"Come on now. You know that I know that you're lying."

"Can we just walk in silence please? We don't have to talk about everything, Aaron."

The way she kept saying my name with so much emphasis made me feel like I had done something wrong. I quickly retraced my steps for the day. We had done all our homework the night before, and Sasha wasn't at school that day. I had come to the conclusion that it was not something I did.

"Last time I checked, Kendall, we are best friends, and if I am not mistaken, best friends tell each other *everything*."

I made a grand gesture in an attempt to make her laugh, but I got nothing. She sped up her pace and walked past me. I stopped in my tracks and nodded my head in understanding. She was not in the mood for games. That hurt because usually a well-placed, outlandish gesture would at least get her to smile and then get her talking. My wit was not the victor in this battle.

We finally made it off the school campus, and the silence was killing me. I was having a good day. Melinda Rose, who I had a crush on since the start of the school year, said that she would go to the dance with me. I aced my math and science pop quizzes, and I got an extra sandwich at lunch for free. I hated that I could not share in my mild bliss. "Bobby Sherry asked who you are going to the dance with." Since I knew she did not have a date yet, I figured that would be good news.

Our school dances were a little different than normal schools. Instead of waiting until after school, our dances started during lunch and lasted the duration of the school day. Anybody who did not go to the dance had the options of staying home or staying in class for extra credit. The dance was only for the eighth graders, which made us even more excited to go.

"I'm not going," Kendall murmured.

"What do you mean you're not going?" I almost yelled.

Just the day before we talked about what we were going to wear. Then all of a sudden, she was not going. I was furious. The dance was three weeks away.

"I have some extra credit that I have to do for Mr. Kane's geography class."

"Kendall, you do realize that an A is the highest grade you can get, right?"

My confusion and anger started to get the best of me as I walked past her, speeding up my pace. I got about ten feet in front of her then turned around and walked back to her. I stood in front of her path, causing her not to be able to walk. Every time she would try to walk around me, I would stand in her way. She finally gave up and stood in front of me, looking at the ground.

"I really do not want to talk," she said, not looking up.

I shook my head in rebuttal.

"Well, I guess we are not going home because I am not moving until you tell me what is wrong."

She sighed as she played with the ground with her foot.

"Well, I guess we aren't."

She adjusted her backpack and looked to her left at some of our classmates walking by. She gave them a slight smile before putting her focus back toward the ground.

"Will you look at me? Hell, if you didn't want to talk, you shouldn't have waited on me to get out of practice."

She took a deep breath and looked at me on the brink of tears.

"I don't want you to not be my friend."

I instinctively pulled her into a hug.

"Kendall, what the hell are you talking about? I will always be your friend."

"Aaron, I'm pregnant," she said in my chest.

My eyes got big as I held her tighter. I did not even know that she was sexually active. Frantically saying, "Do your parents know?"

She pulled back and said, "They can't know. They can't find out." She was hysterical.

"Okay, okay. We will figure this out."

I pulled her back into a hug.

The day of the dance seemed like it took forever to come. It was exhausting, trying to keep my grades up, concentrating at practice, and making sure Kendall's secret stayed a secret. The dance was a much-needed break. Knowing that Kendall was not going to be there took a lot of the weight off. Ty, Bobby, and I stood next to the snack table so that we could see all the girls that were there. Melinda Rose cancelled on me a few days before the dance, saying that she was failing one of her classes and needed the extra credit, so she had to stay in class instead of going to the dance. Ty's plans had always been to go to the dance by himself. "One chick is not going to tie me down," was his argument. "If I go solo, I can dance with who I want to and get as many numbers that I want."

We stood, nodding our head to the music with cups of punch in our hand.

"Oh snap, Shalonda Walker just walked in." Ty licked his lips and threw his cup in the trash can beside him. "I will be right back."

Bobby and I laughed as he walked away, bobbing his head to the beat. "I'm going to pee," Bobby said before walking away without me acknowledging his statement. I laughed to myself as I kept nodding my head to the music.

I looked around the crowded gym. There were several people in the middle of the basketball court dancing to the music and some people scattered throughout the bleachers. Most people were coupled up or with their groups of friends, so Sasha stuck out like a sore thumb as she sat by herself. I contemplated if I should talk to her or not. I decided against it as I focused my attention back to the dance floor. As I glanced over the crowd, I saw Melinda Rose dancing with Colby Justice, the quarterback of the football team. My chest tightened as all the anger I had been holding in began to struggle to come out. I threw my drink in the trash as I started to make my way to them.

"As school dances go, this one isn't too bad, huh."

My arm was being pulled back to the spot that I was standing in. I looked back to see Sasha smiling as she gently pulled. I snatched my arm away and turned back toward the dance floor. Melinda and I had locked eyes, and I heard my last name being called.

"What?" I hollered back at Sasha.

"Calm your ass down before you get suspended. We only have three and a half months left."

She did not back down.

"Fuck you talkin' to?" I asked, forgetting about Melinda for a second.

"Somebody about to do something real stupid over a girl who didn't like him to begin with." I looked back at the dance floor and Melinda and Colby weren't there. I sucked my teeth as I started to leave to find them. "Come on, Phillips, don't leave." Sasha came around me, blocking my path. "I came over here because I saw the two of them come in. Everybody knew that she dumped you for him, but I figured you didn't. The look on your face when I got over here let me know that I was right." She was silent for a moment. I suppose waiting on me to say something after her comment, but I did not. "You look like you need to blow off some steam now, so let's dance."

She smiled at me as she pulled me to the crowd. I was hesitant at first, but she started doing the goofiest dance I had ever seen around me, causing me to laugh.

"Okay. Okay. I will dance with you. Just please stop doing that."

I laughed and noticed people noticing her.

"I can do this all day," she joked. I pulled her to me, and we dance regularly for three or four songs. "Man, I'm tired," she said. "I'm about to get something to drink. You want anything?"

"I'll walk with you. I'm a little tired too."

We got our drinks and went to the bleachers to sit down. She sat a bleacher above me, causing me to lean back as we talked.

"Thank you for that." She smiled as she took a drink. "I know we don't really talk. Shoot. I know you don't like me."

I scrunched up my face.

"What you talking 'bout? I never said I didn't like you," I tried to deny.

"Don't play with me, Aaron. You and Kendall have been treating me like a fungus since the first grade."

"If I treated you so bad, why help me?"

She sat, thinking for a moment before answering, "Because you are only a douchebag when Kendall is around." The way we were sitting, Sasha had a view of the gym door. "Speaking of the devil." She scuffed and got up. "See you around, Phillips," she said before walking away.

I looked to where she was just looking and saw Kendall walking in, bobbing her head to the music, speaking to a couple of people that were standing around the door. I laid my head back on the bleachers for a moment, thinking about what Sasha had just said. Kendall and I always fed off each other's energy. Typically, if one of us did not like somebody, that person was instantly the other person's enemy. That's how best friends were supposed to be, right?

"I been lookin' for you, man," Ty said as he took Sasha's place on the bleachers, eating a bag of chips. "You know Kendall is here."

"Yeah, I saw her when she came in. Ty, let me ask you a question." I sat up as I talked. "Do I act different when I'm around Kendall?"

He chuckled and said, "Yeah, but I'm used to it now."

"Hey, why y'all sitting down?" Kendall asked, walking up to us on the bleachers.

"I thought you weren't coming," I said, slightly annoyed.

"Well, class was super boring, and I overheard a couple of the girls in class talking about Melinda and Colby. So I decided since I already bought my ticket, I might as well come and see if I see her on the dance floor."

She smiled as she stood in front of me and Ty. I rolled my eyes.

"You know you can't fight anybody right now. Hell, you barely supposed to be at school." She cut her eyes at me, thinking I was going to let it slip. I forced a smile. "Don't worry about Melinda. I'm not."

Kendall
2015

I do not understand why my mother and Aaron are pushing this so hard. Not all friendships are made to last. Ours just so happened to not be able to stand against distance. Thinking back to the diary entry I had just read moments ago, a part of me knew our friendship wouldn't last.

"What I do know is you both have been acting foolish." She leans on the door as she says, "Aaron, you know that you have always been a second son to me, and I will always love you as such, but right now you have to wake up and see what has been in your face for years."

My eyes widen. What is this woman about to blurt out of her mouth? I hold my breath, waiting for the words to fill the room.

"Kendall has been in love with you since I can remember."

I cannot breathe; I cannot move. Why would she say that out loud? Aaron is a married man. That is not something you tell a married man. My whole body is in a panic. What is he thinking? Maybe he went deaf while she was talking and did not hear her. Maybe I am dreaming? Yes! That's it! *This is a dream, and I am going to wake up any minute.* I closed my eyes. *Any minute, and this will all be over*, I say to myself. *I will be back in my apartment in North Carolina, sitting on the couch with my cats, Alice and Jim Boy, while laughing with my dad for falling asleep on the phone again.*

"Kendall," his voice pulls me out of my trance.

My mother left the room, leaving us to "figure it out."

"Are you going to say anything?"

I feel my palms getting sweaty and a sudden urge to sit.

I make my way over to the bed before speaking, "Yes, I would like another plate, please. Thank you."

He stares at me in disbelief.

"So you are just going to…"

My solid stare cut him off. He nods his head and moves toward the desk where the plate is still sitting. I have to get myself together before I have this conversation.

I scoot toward the top of the bed to grab my cell phone that I had placed there when I came in the room. I put it there on silent in hopes to not be bothered. Clearly, that did not work. *I know you are here. Get in here now*, I text and put my phone back on the nightstand.

"I will be back. When I come back, we will have this conversation."

I try to acknowledge his statement as he leaves the room, but every word I can say is caught in my throat. A shot of Jack Daniels would be amazing right now.

No sooner than the door closes, it swiftly opens again. The look on her face is a mixture of shock and admiration as she watched him walking down the hall.

"Damn, he still looks good," she says, closing the door.

"More than good," I say in agreement, my face still as blank as when my mother spoke.

"I got your text… What's going on? It was super cryptic and super demanding. Shoot, you got me rushing in here past all those fine men. I know this is a funeral, but I'm trying to find me another husband."

I laugh as she sits on my bed matter-of-factly.

"Sasha, shut up. Tony is not letting your ass go anywhere."

She rolls her eyes as I speak her truth.

"But a girl can dream, right?"

I shake my head and get right into my dilemma.

"So my mom told him," I say, playing with my freshly manicured fingers.

"Kendall, now you know I have never been good at word games and cracking clues. I need you to speak English to me."

This time I roll my eyes.

"Aaron," I say, looking at her.

"Aaron what?" she asks, not putting two and two together.

I take a deep sigh and shake my head. I have to say this out loud. I have to hear my actual voice speak the words. It will not be in my head anymore; meaning it is real and in the atmosphere.

I look down at my hands and mumble, "My mom told Aaron that I am in love with him."

Sasha pushes herself away from me.

"I'm sorry, what?" I can hear that she is trying to hold back her laughter. "Kendall Lancaster, I know damn well Aaron is not just finding out how you feel about him." I do not reply. "What?" she questions before letting her laugh out. "I'm sorry, I don't mean to laugh. I just thought that was the reason you two stopped talking in college."

I shake my head.

"I can't do this, Sasha. I have to leave. I can't stay here. He is going to come back, and he is going to want to talk. He is going to want an explanation, and I don't have one. Not now, not today."

She pulls me into a hug as I try to keep my composure.

"Okay, calm down. You got this." She rubs my back as I lay my head on her shoulder. "Why have you never told him?"

"It was never the right time." I shrug.

She pulls me away from her and looks me dead in my eyes.

"You are telling me the man that you are in love with decides to walk his ass down the aisle with some other chick, and you couldn't find the right time to break that shit up?"

I've tried for years not to imagine his wedding day. The fact that we have the same friends, and all of them were in attendance and plastered the event on Shadow made it hard to ignore.

"He seemed happy, Sash. Who am I to come in between a man in love?"

"Maybe the woman he is in love with. Kendall, a blind man could see that that man was in love with you. Hell, Melanie knew it."

I shake my head in disbelief. That cannot be true. I know Aaron, and if that is how he was feeling, he would have said something.

"When Aaron and I were together in high school, I saw it. Why do you think I broke up with him? I was never going to be you, and I understood that."

I shake my head once again in disbelief and said, "I'm sorry, Sash, I just do not believe you."

She laughs at my stubbornness.

"What I do not believe is how the two of you have been so blind. But I digress. It's clearly too late for all of that now anyway, right," she states as she stands and walks over to the window. "I miss looking out of this window when I would spend the night. It was so calming."

I smiled. "I know, right. Us up all night prank-calling people."

We laugh. She turns toward me and said, "Things were so simple then."

My eyes divert to the floor. Simple is not what I would call my childhood.

"Yeah. How are the kids? Did you bring them?" I change the subject. This walk down memory lane is not one that I want to take today.

"They're good. Downstairs eating everything they can get their grubby, little hands on." I chuckle. "Once you get everything situated up here, I'm sure they would love to see their Auntie Ken."

I nod, saying, "It has been a few months, huh?"

She laughs and wittily states, "You say that like you live right up the street." She sat back on the bed opposite of where I am sitting.

"I know, but I feel like I should see them more. You all should come up for Christmas. I know you need a getaway, and I could use the company." I smile, hoping for a yes. "Sleepover old-school style."

I really miss my friend. Since Aaron and I were not talking, I really needed somebody to feel that void. I needed a level head. Although Sasha and I became friends in high school, after Aaron met Melanie, we really grew close as friends. I would often think back to what Aaron once said, "You and Sasha are the same person. You are just more reckless and stubborn." I would always shake my head and laugh. People say that you cannot get along with people who are just like you, but for some reason, Sasha and I work.

"I'm sure we can work something out," she says as my bedroom door opened after a light knock. I shake my head as Aaron enters the room uninvited, again. Sasha stands and stretches. "Well, I will let you two talk."

"But I wasn't done talking to you," I say pouting. "Come on sit back down. Aaron can come back later."

Sasha laughs and says, "You do not need me to tell you anything you don't already know. You both know what you want to say, so say it already."

She comes around the bed and kisses Aaron on the cheek before leaving the room, closing the door behind her.

As soon as the door closes, it feels like Sasha has taken all the air with her. I cannot look at him. I know that as soon as I do, my mother's words will be truly real and in the open. I put my head in my hands to gather my thoughts. I hear the fresh plate being set on the desk, taking the place of where the previous one once stewed. Then I heard the chair crack, letting me know that Aaron had picked his battleground. I think back to what Sasha had just said about him being in love with me too. I wonder what that could mean for our friendship now. If it is true, is he still in love with me?

"So?" his voice breaks the silence.

I move my hands to look at him. He leans back in the chair, flashing a cocky smile. I shake my head and suck my teeth. He is enjoying this entirely too much.

"So," I mock, rolling my eyes. "Thank you for making me another plate."

I get up to retrieve the plate from the desk, but he moves it closer to him. I attempt to reach around him, but he stops me.

"Oh no. We are not going to pretend that your mom did not just come in here and drop a bomb."

I move closer to him to try to get around him to get the plate.

"I don't know what you are talking about."

He gets up, clearly annoyed, and pushed the plate to the back of the desk—out of my reach—then sits in front of it to make sure there is no confusion that I will not be eating until we have this conversation.

"I have been in love with you since the tenth grade." I step away from him, shock covering my face. He grabs my hand, pulling me back toward him. "I have been in love with you since the tenth grade. From then on, it seemed like every girl that I talked to, every girl that I dated, every girl that I saw on the street I compared to you. Is she going to understand exactly what I am thinking or feeling without me saying a word? Is she always going to have my back no matter what? You have always been my beautiful rock that I never wanted to lose."

My heartbeat seems to speed up with every word not with lust or love but with anger.

"If this is how you felt, why did you get married?" I snatched my hand away. "Why push me away for her? You cannot stand here and tell me that you love me when you made the choice. You chose who you wanted to be with."

When I woke up this morning, I knew today was going to be hard. I knew that I might run into everything that I was running from. I thought that I would see Aaron, and it would be a quick, "Hey, how are you?" and we would move on, and I would be able to avoid my brother. That would have been the perfect day for today. Me starting to get an unbearable headache was not a part of the plan.

"So, all of this is my fault, huh?" He folds his arms across his chest. "How many times did I ask you about Melanie? And how many times did you say, 'I like her for you.'?" He attempts to mimic me.

I roll my eyes, remembering our conversations and lying through my teeth.

"I can only go by what you tell me, Kendall."

"I was being a good friend and trying not to show my jealousy. But how am I supposed to feel when I tell you that I need you to come help me with a situation, and you never showed up? Or when I'm stranded on the side of the road because I was coming to see you, and you never showed up? Or you leaving me in your apartment for a week when I came to see you? From my point of view, you had already made up your mind." I sit on the bed, shaking my head, and look up at him. "I have been in love with you since we were thirteen. I figured if we could still be friends, after my scare, I didn't want anybody else in my corner."

He drops his head then wipes his face with both hands. I can hear his phone vibrating in his pocket. He pulls it out of his pocket, looks at it, and sighs. He looks at me, and I wave him away.

"Go ahead. Don't let me stop you now."

I watch the debate that is clearly going on in his head, on his face. The phone stops vibrating and instantly starts again.

"I'm sorry, Ken—"

I cut him off, "Just go."

I move from the bed back to the window seat.

Tenth Grade, 2000
Aaron
Age Fourteen

Sasha and I sat at the top of the bleachers in the gym, waiting on the bell to ring. It was the third day of classes, and Sasha was the only person that I talked to in this class. Most of the school knew me from playing basketball, but I tried to keep to myself most of the time. The school's female population noticed me about halfway through the last school year. Our homecoming game I scored the winning shot. From then on, I was like a celebrity. Kendall would tell me all the time how she would get dirty looks in the hallways because people thought that we were together. I always thought that was funny.

"I think I'm going to try out for cheerleading this year," Sasha announced as she doodled in her notebook.

"You should. You got the body for it." I leaned back to try to see what she was drawing. "What's that?" I asked, pulling the notebook down so that I could get a better view. She snatched the notebook away, pulling it closer to her.

"Get out my business."

I sucked my teeth.

"You ain't got no business. Let me see." I reached for it again, and she moved away from me, grabbing her backpack as she moved. "Fine, be like that. I don't want to see your stupid picture no way," I joked as she rolled her eyes. She closed her notebook and set it on the bleachers beside her. "You going to Kendall's house today?" I asked to change the subject.

"I might, I don't know yet. You know my mom be tripping sometimes."

I nodded and said, "Me and Ty might go over there."

"To play the game?"

Kendall's dad bought her a PlayStation for Christmas last year. Ty and I have been at her house every day since.

"That isn't the only reason," I said mockingly.

"Okay, so give me another reason," she challenged.

"Because she's my friend, duh," I joked, causing her to laugh.

"I've known both of you for a long time, and it always seemed like more than just friends to me."

I looked at her, confused, and laughed.

"Out of all these chicks here, I thought you would be the one to see it."

She nodded her head clearly, not understanding what I was saying.

Even when Kendall and Sasha did not get along, I still talked to Sasha. We would also hang out from time to time. We would have study sessions together, which made me curious about her. If she was not at school or studying, she was making sure her sister and brother were taken care of. She invited me over once to study while her mom was at work. We barely got any studying done because she was checking their homework, making sure the chores were done, and making sure everybody ate before her mom came home. I was amazed. The only thing I did when I got home was dive in the bed. I grew to admire her strength and how she made it seem like it did not phase her.

"I knew it was something between you two," she said.

I slid over to where she moved and moved up to the bleacher next to her. I caressed her cheek as I pulled her in to whisper in her ear.

"I'm not checkin' for her cause I've been checkin' for you."

I ran my hand down her cheek as I watched her melt. She quickly snapped back to herself.

"Aaron, don't play with me," she said as the bell rang.

"I don't have a single reason to lie to you. I want you. If you don't want me, then say so, and this conversation can end right now."

She stared at me as everybody around us cleared out, and more people came in for their class.

"I had no idea this is how you felt. I mean, of course, I like you too."

I smiled.

"So you want to be my girl?"

She blushed and nodded her head. I smiled from ear to ear. I was excited. I've had girlfriends before, but none that I was actually excited to be with.

"Well, come on and let me walk my girl to class," I said, standing up.

She blushed as she gathered her things. She stood beside me.

"I like the way you said that," she said and smiled.

"What's that?"

"Your girl," she said as she walked down the bleachers, giggling.

As we walked to her next class, I made it a point to put my arm around her shoulders. Everybody could see that we were a couple. Sasha giggled and smiled as we saw everybody's reaction. Sasha was easily one of the best-looking girls at the school, so the guys' approval was very apparent. We reached her class, and I gave her a hug before leaving. Kendall and I had the next class together, and I could not wait to tell her. I walked in to find Kendall already sitting on my desk with her arms folded across her chest. A couple of girls were snickering as I walked past. Kendall stared at me through narrow eyes as I smiled from ear to ear.

"Man, put that Colgate up," she demanded as I reached my desk. "How you not going to tell me you had a thing for Sasha?

I mean, I'm cool with the heffa now, but dang. You could've given me a heads up."

I sat in my seat as she got off the desk, talking to me. I shook my head.

"How you find out so fast?" I asked, genuinely curious.

I knew that news traveled fast, but that was lightning speed. She moved toward her seat on the other side of the room as she spoke.

"You know your groupies know everything."

She smiled as she reached her desk.

"I have no idea what you are talking about."

As she sat at her desk, she nodded her head toward the girls that giggled as I came in class. I nodded my head, understanding.

Class let out, and Kendall waited for me outside of the classroom door, handing me a note. We learned the hard way that passing notes in class was not a good idea. Tera Coleman decided that she did not want to pass my note to Kendall in the eighth grade. Instead she decided to read it herself. Luckily, it was not anything bad. Kendall was just reminding me to bring a change of clothes to her house that weekend. I believe, that was when the rumors about Kendall and I got started.

"You don't have to write back if you don't want to. I'll see you after school."

She walked off before I could reply. I put the note in my pocket and went to my next class.

Aaron
2015

I come back into the room and see her sitting in her favorite place by the window. I close the door, making my presence known.

"I don't want you here anymore."

She does not turn around, but I can tell that she is crying. Seeing her cry has always broken my heart.

"Ken, I want to talk this out."

She gets up and looks at me.

"That's the thing, Aaron. I don't. I want to act on what I have been feeling for years. But I can't. I never could. It was always something, and then there was Levi…" She shakes her head and sits on her bed, facing the window. "You remember the note that I gave you when you and Sasha first started talking?"

I rack my brain, trying to remember the note that she is referring to.

"We passed so many notes in school," I say, sitting on the bed, close to the door.

As our backs face each other, I feel the bed move then look beside me. There is an old, folded piece of paper sitting beside me on the bed. The only reason I know that it is older because of the color of the paper. It is a dirty-yellow color. Other than that, it looks as though it has not been touched.

"We met after school, and you said that you forgot that I gave it to you. I was relieved. When you fell asleep at my house that evening, I found it in your jacket pocket."

I look at her, confused, and ask, "And you kept it all these years?"

She chuckles a little then says, "I figured one day I would muster up the courage to give it to you. I almost did so many times, but I was scared of how you would react. I was scared of losing my friend. It's funny because not telling you caused what I feared anyway."

I sigh as I pick up the paper from the bed.

"I have to use the restroom. I will be back." She stands to walk out of the room.

"You just don't want to watch me read it," I joke, causing her to laugh a little.

"Or I have to pee," she says before leaving the room.

I chuckle as I unfold the paper.

The inside of the paper did not match the outside coloring. I can tell that it has not been opened since it was folded. Although I already knew the gist of what the note says, something about reading it takes me back to high school, back to being the lanky teenage boy trying to catch the eye of his best friend to no avail. I open the note all the way and chuckle. "Aug. 24, 2000," is written at the top-right corner of the paper, as if it was to be turned in for an assignment. I asked her once why she always dated our notes. She said, "Memories, duh! One day we are going to come across our notes and laugh at how crazy we are. With the date, there we can see the progression of our crazy." I get to the body of the note and start reading.

> *I want to start off by saying that I'm not mad that you chose Sasha over me. Just a little disappointed. I know that I haven't openly said it. I guess I thought that you would figure it out and I wouldn't have to, but here it is. I'm in love with you, Aaron. I have been for a long time, and not being able to tell you that has been killing me. I hope that you feel the same. If you don't, then I hope we can still be friends. All I want is for you to be happy.*

I finish reading and set the paper back on the bed beside me. I wonder what it would have been like if Kendall and I had gotten together back then. I honestly think that we would still be together. I realized that I was in love with Kendall when Sasha and I broke up. Sasha was the one who broke it off with me, saying that she was too busy to be a good girlfriend. I think she knew that I was in love with Kendall.

I lay back on the bed with my eyes closed. Many nights I have laid wondering what seeing Kendall again would be like. This reality was not one of the scenarios that I came up with. Hearing Kendall say how much I left her hanging while we were in college brought a lot more clarity to why she had stopped talking to me. I was a shitty friend. It went from talking at least twice a week, to her not answering my calls, to saying she would call me back and never do, to no communication at all. I know people grow apart, but not us, not the friendship that we had. I guess I was so caught up in Melanie that I put the most important person in my life on the backburner. I never thought that putting it on the backburner would completely freeze it.

I quickly jump up to a seated position as I hear a loud bang on the door then a male voice.

"You not going to speak to your big brother?"

I stand, recognizing Levi's now-husky voice. His voice has changed a little throughout the years. He now had that "I smoke ten packs of cigarettes a day" voice, but there is no doubt that it is him.

"Levi, I just want to be left alone." Her voice is so sheepish it is almost unrecognizable.

"Aw, come on now. I miss my little sister. And my dad just died. I need somebody to console me."

I open the door, causing Kendall to fall back into my chest. It looks as though he has her pinned on the door.

"She said she wants to be left alone," I say as she goes under my arm that is holding open the door.

"Yet you are here."

He straightens his posture as he speaks. He seems a little taller than I remember. He is almost eye level to my six-foot-three-inch frame. My instinct to protect Kendall kicks in as we stare at each other.

"We both know how this is going to go, Levi. Just walk away," I say, referring to our last encounter.

College, 2004
Aaron
Age Twenty

I went home the summer of my sophomore and junior year in college. This was around the time Kendall and I had not talked for a while. The last time that I talked to her she told me that she was not going to go home. I was surprised when she called and asked me to help her move some things at her mom's house. I was more than happy to help because I missed her, and I had so much that I wanted to tell her. When I got there, Levi was pulling up at the same time. I turned the music down in my 1999 Toyota Camry and rolled my eyes. I already knew he was about to start something. I got out of the car, trying to ignore the fact that I heard his car door close right after mine.

"Say, man, you know better than to come to my mama's house playin' all that loud music. This here is a respectable neighborhood," he announced, walking up behind me.

He sounded as if he was in his forties instead of a twenty-five-year-old.

"Man, I'm not here to start shit with you."

I did not turn to acknowledge him. I kept walking toward the carport door. This clearly irritated him.

"You look a man in his eyes when you talk to him, boy."

He stood in front of me, causing me to stop walking.

Around my eleventh-grade year was when I had grown taller than Levi. He did not seem to care. In fact, I think it made him hate me more, which I found to be rather amusing. Sometimes if he was at their dad's house, I would purposefully reach for something high up the cabinet because I knew he could not reach it. He was not really that much shorter than me, but the height advantage was very apparent.

"When I see one, I will be sure to do that."

I looked past him as I talked. He sucked his teeth in agitation.

"I don't even know why you're here. Kay not even here."

I walked around him, ignoring his inquiry. I am sure Kendall purposefully did not tell him that she was home.

"Say, man, don't you walk away from me when I'm talkin' to you."

I still did not reply as he hollered behind me. Before I knew it, I was jilted to the ground. Levi had tackled me from behind, causing me to crease my white Air Force 1s. Up until this moment, Levi had never actually put his hands on me. It was always just threats. I guess this day he felt bold enough to act on his challenges. I looked at my shoes first then noticed his fist coming for my head and landed on its target—my eye. If I was not already mad that sent me over the edge. I managed to get myself to my feet and tackle him to the ground. My fist did not stop punching his face until their neighbor, Mr. White, pulled me away.

Mr. White was an older white man who lives to the right of Kendall's mom, Ms. Cynthia. On appearance, he didn't look like he had much of anything, just a middle-aged man who was beginning to bald at the top of his head. That day I learned that he was actually quite muscular. He pulled me off Levi with ease.

"You two know better than this," Mr. White stated, referring to watching us grow up.

I snatched away from him and started to get back in my car. Kendall and Ms. Cynthia ran out of the house as I reached the car door.

"Oh my god! What happened?" Ms. Cynthia hollered as she ran to Levi.

Kendall ran behind, slightly grinning as she noticed the scene. She ran up to me and touched my face, causing me to swat her hand away.

"Hold still," she demanded while forcing me down to her level so that she could get a better look at the damage. "It's going to be bruised and sore for a few days, but nothing too bad." She moved my head from side to side as she talked.

"What happened?" Ms. Cynthia questioned again as she helped Levi off the ground.

"Man, Ma, I don't even know. I pulled up, and next thing I know he was on top of me. I told you to stop letting him come around here."

Ms. Cynthia looked confused.

"What? That doesn't sound like you at all, Aaron."

I started to holler back in my defense when Mr. White stepped in, "Mr. Levi, I don't know where you pull these lies from, but you tell your mother the truth right now. You are too old to be out here acting like this."

Levi did not say anything as Ms. Cynthia looked at him, waiting for his response. She looked at me, and I did not say anything either. I guess the anger had my tongue. Mr. White shook his head in both disbelief and disappointment.

"I was watching from my kitchen window as they both pulled up. Levi got out of the car, hollering at Aaron about his music"—he looked at me—"which was not that loud, by the way." He looked back at Ms. Cynthia. "Next thing I know, Levi is launching at Aaron."

Ms. Cynthia looked at Levi, causing him to cower.

"Get in the house," she spoke through her teeth. Levi obeyed as he stomps into the house. "Thank you, Roger. I'm glad you were watching."

"Ma, me and Aaron are going to leave for a little while. Let him calm down," Kendall said as she pulled me toward the passenger side of my car.

Ms. Cynthia nodded her head as she continued talking to Mr. White.

Kendall
2015

I watch from behind Aaron as they exchanged stares.

"That's okay," Levi says as he breaks the staring contest. "I'll be back later."

He licks his lips as he walks away. I thought all that was over. In the eleventh grade was when I got my first real boyfriend. I have no idea how he found out, but he cornered me at my dad's house, saying, "I hope you learn how to keep your legs closed. If not, at least you already know what to do," with a devilish smile, as if he accomplished something.

Aaron closes the door as Levi walks off.

"What is his problem?" he asks, turning around.

I lose all control as he faces me. I feel myself pulling Aaron into a kiss. To my surprise, he does not break away but pulls me in tighter. Our bodies, our lips feel like they belong together.

He had always been my hero, my protector. When he was around, there was no harm that came to me, not from Levi or anyone else. I used to kick myself for not telling him everything. I am honestly not sure what would have happened. Our friendship was so strong, but I thought that every little thing would cause us not to be friends anymore. When I told him I was pregnant in the eighth grade, he stayed with me every step of the way while my Aunt Lisa took me to get an abortion. I assumed she thought that it was Aaron's. Aaron and I said nothing to make her think otherwise. It surprised me the most when he never asked who the father was. I believe if he would have asked, then I would have told him.

I break the kiss and move away.

"You really need to leave," I say.

Again, I do my best not to look at him or make eye contact. I put my hands up to my lips to make sure this is not a dream. My curiosity is satisfied with a tingling bliss. Before I can reach my lips, he pulls me back in to him. I feel my frame being engulfed in his arms once again. If he was not holding me, I am sure I would have melt. His lips feel like electric pillows as he attacks my lips. I put my arms around his neck, cupping the back of his head to pull him in closer. He picks me up, and I instinctively put my legs around his waist. He leads us to the bed as I feel his phone vibrate in his pants pocket. He does not break his stride as his right hand follows my leg up my dress and lands on my thigh. The vibration stops then starts again. He once again ignores the phone as he moves from my lips to my neck. I let out a hushed moan as his lips and tongue caresses my left jugular. His hand moves up to my waist. The vibration stops again. He moves his lips down to my chest. I lightly scratch his back under his shirt as I let out another moan, this time slightly louder. His phone starts vibrating again. This time he removes the phone from his pocket and tosses it to the other side of the room.

"Oops," he said, causing me to giggle as the phone hit the carpeted floor.

He looks down at me, smiling, causing me to melt all over again. He leans back down to meet my lips. Placing his hand back on my thigh, he gently rubs back up to my waist. He moves it around my hip, finding my right cheek and caressing it.

All the years I have been intimate, I have never felt what I am feeling now. I have never felt the butterflies that I am feeling in my stomach. I have never felt the electricity, between him and I, with anybody else. It took me years to even want to have sex with anybody. When I did, it felt like nothing. I liked the guys I was with. I thought I might have loved one or two, but none of them ever made me feel the way Aaron is now. Just his touch is making me want to rip both our clothes off, but we cannot do this.

"Aaron, wait," I say between kisses.

"Why?"

He moves back down to my neck.

I close my eyes tight before speaking, "Because you're married."

I move my hand from under his shirt. He exhales and plops down on top of me, defeated.

"Yes, I am." He rolls to the right side of me, but not moving his hand from under my dress. I do not protest. "To the wrong person."

We both stare at the ceiling for a moment.

"Did you know that before you got married?"

I believe I know the answer, but I want to hear him say it.

"Yeah," he says plainly.

The room falls silent again until the vibration of his phone startled me a little. He sighs and starts to get up to get it. I roll toward him, putting my hand on his chest.

"Leave it," I say, contradicting my initial protest.

He smiles as he lays back down, pulling me toward him.

"I love you, Kendall."

These words I have heard from him many times. I know he loves me, but this one is different. It means something different. I look at him, into the eyes that I have been avoiding since he came in the room.

"I love you too, Aaron."

Our lips meet once again. This time instead of lust, it is slow and full of passion.

College, 2005
Kendall
Age Twenty-One

David and I met while I was walking back to my dorm. I had been to a couple of basketball games, so I knew who he was. He was not the star player, but he got his time on the court. He stood about six feet, three inches, and he shared the same complexion as me. His braces made his lips poke out a little farther than what they probably should have, but I did not mind. They were still nice and full. He wore his hair in shoulder-length dreadlocks. It seemed like he always kept them freshly twisted and pulled back out of his face. When I would see him around campus, he was always well-dressed, very preppy with slacks and a button-down. The night we met was no different.

It was my senior year, and I decided not to go home on Christmas break to try to stay away from any and all drama. My mother and dad were uncharacteristically at each other's throat. Avoiding Levi had always been my life mission. And after the last time Aaron said he was going to visit and did not show, or even call to apologize, I made up my mind that that would be our last conversation. I had just finished getting me a turkey sandwich, chips, and orange soda from the campus convenience store and headed back to my room to watch *The Polar Express*. Even though I was not at home, I was still in the Christmas spirit. His first words were, "You're too cute to look so sad."

When the semester started, David and I had been dating for almost two months. I liked him a lot. He kept my mind off my home issues. My roommate, Josette, found out that he and I were hanging out about a week after the semester started. She almost burst my eardrums from her squeals after walking in on us watching TV. She said she had had a crush on him since she saw him coming from one of his games the semester before. This made her stick around the room a lot more than usual, not giving me and David much alone time.

After about three months, he and I became the "it" couple on campus. It was weird for me to go from being almost invisible to everybody knowing my name. Back home everybody already knew who I was because we grew up together. At school I could walk around, and maybe one or two people knew my name. David and I would walk around, smiling and waving as if we knew every person that spoke. It was truly exhausting.

"Kendall," David questioned.

We sat in his room, attempting to watch whatever was on the five stations that his TV could receive. It was more so watching me as I was falling asleep, lying next to him.

"Yeah." I opened my eyes. "I'm not sleep, you are."

He chuckled as I sat up in an attempt to wake myself.

"Kendall, you know I like you a lot."

I started getting annoyed because I already knew where the conversation was going.

"Why do you want to ruin a good day, David?"

He sighed and countered, "So I can't tell you how I feel?"

"Not if it leads to where it has been for the past two weeks, no." I got off the bed and started to gather my things. "If you want me to leave, all you had to do was say so."

He got off the bed and stopped me from getting my jacket from his desk chair.

"Wait. Wait." He held my hand then pulled me toward him. "I apologize. It was not my intent to upset you. This isn't about sex. I genuinely want you to know that I'm falling for you. You aren't like any other girl I have been with. You're your own woman, and I like that."

I blushed as he held me tighter, causing me to wrap my arms around him.

"I like you a lot too, David. I enjoy spending time with you. You know how to get me out of my head and enjoy the moment."

He leaned down and kissed me. Although his lips were full, to me, his kisses were sloppy. I kissed back the best way I could without showing disgust. His attempt to deepen the kiss made me more turned off. I broke the kiss and smiled an uncomfortable smile.

"I am going to have to leave soon. Can we just find something to watch and chill?"

I moved back to the bed.

"Yeah, sure." He followed, clearly disappointed.

The basketball team had a nine o'clock curfew. It was an hour before campus curfew. I guess the coach did not want them getting caught in anything crazy. It was 7:45 p.m., which meant I had a little over an hour before I had to leave.

We finally settled on *Law & Order* and got comfortable on the bed. He laid behind me as I curled up close to him. His warmth felt good as the room was a little chilly. He played in my hair, which both felt good and tickled a little.

"You finish your history paper?" I questioned, remembering that it was due in a couple of days.

"Almost. I have two paragraphs left. Just have to figure out how to finish it with a bang. Put a little *umph* in it."

He nudged as he *umphed*, causing me to giggle.

"I'm sure your professor will find that entertaining."

"What can I say. I'm Mr. Entertaining."

I could feel his smile as I turned to look at him. A silly grin was plastered across his face. I laughed. As I turned back toward the TV, he turned my head back toward him, pulling me into a kiss. This time the kiss was not as juicy but a little more forceful. He rolled over on top of me, pushing his tongue in my mouth. I really liked David, but kissing was not his strong suit. He started fondling my chest, which actually felt nice. I moaned softly as he sucked on my neck. He reached around and unhooked my bra with one hand then moved back around to my chest. He lifted my shirt, exposing my breast to the chill air. He started giving both breasts equal attention. While sucking one, he would massage the other. He sucked on the right side, and his left hand trailed down my stomach to the waist of my green sweatpants.

He slid his hand down further, and I froze. I could not move. If I made a noise, I would get in trouble. No, I had to be quiet. "Just lay there and take it," Levi's voice echoed in my head. "You like it. Don't fight it." I could feel the tears streaming down, but I could not move. Even after David realized something was not right, I could not move.

I could hear myself repeating, "I'm sorry. It won't happen again," at a low whisper. Couldn't be too loud. Being loud made it worse. "I'm sorry," I heard myself cry as I did many times before.

"What is happening?" David questioned, clearly confused. "Kendall, what's wrong?"

I could not answer. Can't be too loud.

"I'm sorry," I said again through tears.

"Hello, Josette. It's David. I don't know who else to call. Something is wrong with Kendall."

I missed the remainder of that semester. Nobody was able to calm me down. I was sent to a psychiatric hospital where they had to sedate me for three days. My parents had to be called because I had not said much of anything; all they were told was I was suffering from some type of sexual trauma. When I was able to communicate, I did not want to talk to anybody. I was so embarrassed. I believed that it was all my fault.

My parents thought it would be better to move me to a hospital closer to home, Prairie View Psychiatrics. The name pretty much described the surroundings. It was in the middle of nowhere. For miles, all you could see was land filled with wildflowers and patches of forest. My parents came to visit every Sunday for the three months I was there. It was two months before I spoke.

"Please don't tell anybody I'm here."

My voice sounded almost unrecognizable as I sat on my bed. My mother sat in a rocking chair in the far-left corner, reading *The Bible* aloud. She almost dropped the book as the light, raspy words were spoken.

"Keith," she said as she got up from her seat.

She did not have to call his name because as soon as I spoke, he turned to face me from the window that faced one of the vast fields. My mother came and sat on the bed beside me as my dad stood the opposite side, demanding answers.

"Who did this to you? Was it one of those college boys? Just give me a name," he fumed.

"Keith, please."

I could not tell them that this was all my fault. If I had just listened to Levi and kept my legs closed, we would not be here. I wanted to, but I could not cry. The only thing I could muster to say was, "Please don't tell anybody I am here." My mother rubbed my back and fixed my hair.

"We won't, sweetie. We just want you to get better. That is all we are wanting right now. Right, Keith?" He huffed and returned back to the window. I knew that him not knowing was hurting him. "Do you want anything? Are you hungry? I can bring you some pie next week."

I wanted to smile but could not. I did not respond. Just look down at the pink-and-blue comforter on the bed.

"Aaron has been asking about you." My eyes widened. "Don't worry. He doesn't know anything. He just knows that you are in the hospital, but not receiving visitors."

"Please…"

"Please what, Kendall?" My dad turned around with tears streaming down his face.

"Keith, not now. She just started talking. Giver her time." She got up to console him.

"I just want to know who hurt my baby girl," he cried.

I could not look at my daddy cry.

I had only seen him cry one other time, when my grandma passed. I was about four or five, but it stood out to me. My dad was six feet even and very stalky. He looked as though if he did not work in construction; he might have played professional football. I believed my dad to be a nice-looking man. The women around the neighborhood sure seemed to think so. Every other day some lady was getting her mail in a way-too-short robe, telling my dad how fine he was that day, and if he needed anything at all, he knew where they lived. I would always pretend like I did not hear them, as most of them were married. I always admired my dad and his quick charm, which was why seeing him cry hurt so bad. Both times.

I left the hospital and stayed with my dad. He felt like he could better protect me if I was living back under his roof. Levi decided at the beginning of the year that he wanted to move to Florida. Something about being a club promoter. Had he had still been living at my mom's, I was not sure what would have happened. Within the first week of me moving back in with my dad, Ty and Sasha were knocking at my door. I watched them walk up from my window seat. Although I did not want to see anybody, I was happy to see friendly faces. They did not bother to knock on the door. Sasha was the first in the room, running over and pulling me into a hug. I smiled weakly as she held on tight.

"Don't you ever in your life scare us like that again."

"Let the girl breathe, dang." Ty laughed.

She let go, and I got up to give Ty a hug.

"How you feelin'?" he asked, breaking the embrace.

I returned to my seat, Ty sat at the desk, and Sasha sat on the bed.

"As good as expected, I suppose."

"What happened? All I know is I got a call from Aaron saying that you were in the hospital, but that is all."

I sat back and looked out of the window. I watched the cars pass by as I talked.

"School just got to be too much, I suppose."

There was a silence. I supposed they were waiting on me to continue with what happen, but I did not.

"Have you talked to Aaron?" Ty asked.

I did not change my position.

"Haven't spoken to him in close to a year."

"I'll rephrase my question. Why haven't you talked to Aaron?" His tone was slightly stern.

"If that is why you are here, then you can leave."

"No. We are here for you." Sasha shifted herself on the bed. "Stop it, Ty. Do you need anything?"

I shook my head, finally acknowledging them.

"Just rest, I suppose. My doctor has me on some kind of mood stabilizers. I don't like how they make me feel. I feel numb. I am a human. I'm supposed to have emotions, but right now I can't even cry if I want to. This is not normal."

Ty sucked his teeth then left the room.

"He is having a hard time with all of this. He feels like if you and Aaron were still talking, this would not have happened."

I shook my head and rolled my eyes.

"Aaron doesn't have a thing to do with any of this. Talking to him would be nice, but I'm okay with not." I looked back out the window. "I don't want to talk about Aaron anymore."

Aaron
2015

I pull her to me as our bare bodies touch. As wrong as the situation is, it feels so right to be lying here with Kendall. She lays on my arm as I play with her now ponytail.

"My food is cold," she says in my neck.

"That's what microwaves are made for."

She chuckles, placing her hand on my face.

"I should have called."

Her voice vibrates on my neck as she moves her hand from my face to my chest.

"We both made mistakes. We can't play the shoulda-coulda-woulda game now."

"You're right, but where do we go from here?"

She kisses my neck and places her leg on mine, pulling our bodies closer together. I feel myself getting excited again.

"Careful. You 'bout to start a second round."

She moves from my neck to my ear.

"Is that a bad thing?" she asks then moves back to my neck.

"Shit," I whisper.

Finally, being in bed with her is like ecstasy on another level. I do not ever want to stop or leave this bed. As if our bodies were not already close enough, I pull her in closer. She looks at me, and I kiss her, trying to convey all my feelings and emotions in that one kiss. I roll over so that I am now on top of her, breaking our kiss to explore her body once more. She pulls me back up to meet her eyes. She smiles as she caresses my face. I put my hand over hers as I kiss her palm.

"I missed you too." She smiles but looks like she is on the brink of tears. "What's wrong? Did I do something wrong?" I ask.

She giggles as she removes her hand from mine to wipe the tear that has just fallen.

"Not at all, Aaron. You are perfect. Always have been. And to know this is what I've been missing." She trails down my chest.

"Phew!" I lick my lips and smile.

"I just never knew that this could feel so good...so..."

She does not finish what she is saying. It seems like she has zoned out. I sit there for a moment, thinking that she is joking and will come back with a witty joke, but she does not. I return to where I was just lying beside her, realizing something is not right. I place my hand on her face, causing her to look at me, but she does not respond. Worry and panic starts, but I keep my composure.

"Kendall, baby, you okay? Talk to me."

She takes a deep breath as she blinks, seemingly trying to focus. I sit us both up in the bed. She looks around, confused, then looks at me.

"Aaron! I'm so sorry. I'm sorry."

I pull the blanket over her exposed body.

"What just happened?" I ask softly.

I had never seen her act like that before. Her eyes were blank, almost glazed over, like she was looking off into space.

"I have to use the bathroom."

She quickly jumps out of the bed, taking the blanket with her to cover her body. I watch her maneuver through the room, trying to find her dress. I sit, befuddled, trying to gather my thoughts and a logical explanation as to what just happen. She finds her dress and puts it on then tries to walk out of the room. I stop her before she is able to leave, blocking the door.

"Hey, hey. Talk to me. What's going on? What just happen?"

She bites her bottom lip as she shakes her head.

"I love you so much, Aaron, but there is so much you don't know. So much that I should have told you a long time ago."

Tears fall as she talks, and I pull her into a hug.

"You can tell me anything. You know that."

She pushes away, looking as if she wants to say something but decides against it.

"I really have to go to the restroom."

I sit back on the bed, angry at myself for letting things go this far. I get up to pick the blanket up off the floor, and I hear my phone vibrating, once again. I sigh as I pick up the phone, answering it while searching for my clothes.

"Hello."

"I have been calling you for hours. Where the hell have you been?" she yells into the phone.

"I will be home soon," I say, unphased by her outrage.

"All caught up with your friend, Kendall?" I do not say anything as I put on my boxers and pants. "I called your mom, and she told me her daddy died."

She spoke in a condescending tone. I still did not answer as I picked up my shirt from the side of the bed by the window. As I pick it up, I see that we had knocked over her diary. It had fallen open facedown.

"Melanie, I will be home soon," I finally say, not answering any of her accusations.

"No! You need to come home now!" she demands as I put on my shirt. I put the phone on the bed as she talks while I find my socks and shoes. "Aaron, I know damn well you did not hang up on me!" she screams loud enough for me to hear her from across the room.

"I'm still here, Melanie, and I told you when I will be home. I have to go now."

I try to end the call.

"Soon is not a damn time," she screams.

I am slightly amused at Melanie's anger. Most of the time I feel like she was intentionally pushing my buttons to get a rise out of me. I do not like getting upset, so when she tries to get a rise, I make it a point to keep my composure. That drives her up a wall, and I secretly love it. I finally find my socks and sit on the bed, putting them on, facing the window. As I am putting my socks and shoes on, I decide to put her diary on her window seat where it usually sit.

I finish putting everything on then pick up the book. Kendall used to guard this thing with her life, so I never thought to ask what was inside. I was sure that, like me, she had some things she did not want me to know. I respected that. Before closing it, I notice that the page it had landed on felt like it had been wet at one point, but dried. I find this to be odd because unless you have spilled a drink or some water on paper, it usually does not warp like this. I turn the book over, figuring that more than likely she spilled a soda or something on it while writing. She was always spilling something. I look at the page and realize how wrong my assumption is. The date on the page read March 2, 1997. I can still hear Melanie's muffled screams through the phone.

"Mel, I'll call you back," I say as I hang up the phone and read

I don't know what I did this time. He came in my room already mad telling me not to make a sound. This time I was ready. Just do what he says and it will be over fast. I got on my knees because I thought I knew what he wanted. But I still can't figure out what I did wrong this time. He laughed at me while he shook his head. He pulled me up by my hair for me to stand up then pushed me on my bed. He said that I was "ready" now.

As I read, I see the pages turn red with anger. How did I not see this? Who is "He"? I keep reading, trying to keep myself together.

He made me lay on my stomach and snatched my shorts and underwear off. It was so hard that the fabric cut my side. It still burns. I didn't understand what was happening until I felt him going…inside…me. It hurt so bad I wanted to scream, but I couldn't. He pushed my head in the mattress as He pumped and whispered in my ear that this was my fault. He is doing this because…

I cannot read anymore. I look back at the date, 1997. We would have been twelve.

"Fuck!" I yell in frustration.

Tears welled up as I look back at what I had just read. Our whole life I made it my mission to make sure that nothing like this happened to her. I knew what guys were saying. I knew how they looked at her. But everyone knew that they would have to get through me first. How the fuck did "He" slip past me?

I flip some pages back to try to see if she wrote his name anywhere. I stop at one of the first entries from June 1993. It was only one sentence.

He made me put it in my mouth while Aaron was here.

College Freshman Year, March 2003
Aaron
Age Eighteen

She sat two seats in front of me in the lecture hall. It was about midspring semester when I noticed her in our African American studies class. I found the class to be very interesting and informative; whereas she did not agree with the way it was being taught, or who was teaching it.

Our professor, Professor Cunningham, was a mid-twenties early thirties Caucasian female with blonde hair and blue eyes. She was actually very knowledgeable about the black culture. She seemed like our history had affected her in some way.

"Man, this is some bull," she randomly spoke out.

"I'm sorry, Ms. Mathis, is there a problem?"

"You want us to believe that you actually care about our history and how we are treated as a people?"

Professor Cunningham looked unphased as she posed the question, "Well, Ms. Mathis, should I not? Should I walk around being a snooty, entitled white woman who only sees the social injustices of the white woman? Or maybe I should use my white privilege to make people think that the way African Americans have been treated is all in the past, and you all should just get over it?" The class was silent as she talked. "Ms. Mathis, black people are not the only people who care about black people."

There were a couple of "oohs" and "awes" as she finished her statement. I looked back at Ms. Mathis as if it was a tennis match, and Professor Cunningham had just served.

The debate lasted the remainder of the class. My fascination would not let me go without meeting Ms. Mathis.

"Excuse me." I jogged to catch up with her. "That was an interesting debate back there," I said, finally catching up.

"No debate. She should not be teaching that class. Period," she fumed, which interested me more.

"Well, let's agree to disagree." I smiled. "My name is Aaron." She gave me a side eye before speeding up her pace. "Can I at least have your name?" I requested as I stopped walking.

She stuck her middle finger up over her shoulder as she walked away, not turning around.

A couple of weeks later, as I was walking out of African American studies class, she caught up with me. Since the dispute with the professor, I made it a point to check to see if she was in class in case of a part two. I did not see her in class that day.

"Hey, Aaron, right?" she asked as she walked beside me, matching my pace.

She was shorter than I remembered. She stood just under my shoulder. She wore her hair in a short pixie cut, which suited her face perfectly. It gave her a more-mature look, which I was certain she was going for. She looked to be mixed, but not with black and white. I couldn't put my finger on what, but she looked more black than the other. If I was not already smitten, her smile pulled me in all the way. Her wide smile took up most of her face and could brighten a room.

"Yes, ma'am. How may I help you?" I smiled back at her.

She had an almost bohemian, carefree feel about her style, reminded me of Freddie from *Different World*.

"I missed class today and was wondering if I could copy your notes." Her smile turned into a plea.

"I don't know," I said, and as I turned my attention forward. If I would have kept looking at her, I would have given up too easily. "There is a lot. And what do you care anyway? Why are you still in the class if you don't agree with it?"

I glanced down at her as she rolled her eyes, causing me to smirk.

"Just because I don't like the teacher does not mean I am going to mess up my chance at the dean's list. Hence the reason why I need your notes. I hear you in class answering questions like you actually study. Unlike half of the class who think they already know what they need to know about our heritage."

My smirk widened as I looked at her.

"So you been checkin' me out?"

Her eyes narrowed as she talked with a half attitude.

"I didn't say all that."

I nodded and joked, "That's okay. I know I look good. But I don't know about those notes though. I mean, how are you supposed to write with only middle fingers?"

She cringed as I finished my statement.

"Yeah, sorry about that. That was a bad day."

I nodded and stopped walking.

"Okay, so let's make a deal." She stopped and looked at me curiously as my smile grew wider. "Let me take you to lunch, and you can have my notes and recording of the lecture."

She smiled back and said, "I don't know. Seems like a steep price just for some notes." She took a step back and looked me over. "But I guess I can make that sacrifice."

I laughed and asked, "You have a class right now?"

Melanie and I made our relationship official a month after we met. I could not wait for Kendall to meet her. Although they were complete opposites, I knew they would get along. Throughout the semester, Kendall and I made it a point to talk at least twice a week. When we did talk, it was mostly me talking about what Melanie and I had done or what we had planned on doing. "I'm happy that she makes you happy," Kendall would say and chuckle at my excitement.

"So your friend Kendall. How long have you two been friends?" Melanie asked one day as we were on our way to the movies.

"Since the second grade. I can't wait for you two to meet." She did not say anything back. "Why you get quiet?"

"Just thinking."

I looked from the road to her them back to the road. Her face was tight. Like she had something to say but was debating saying it. It was an odd face to me because she had never had a problem speaking her mind before.

"About?" I asked, trying to match her sullen attitude.

"I know you two are friends, but to me it seems like more. Like you almost depend on her." I rolled my eyes. "I mean I have friends too, and I do not talk to them nearly as much as you to talk. And the way you talk about her—"

"This is the first and last time I will address this with you," I interrupted clearly annoyed. "Kendall and I have been disbanding this rumor since middle school." We got to the movie theater, and I parked in the first open parking space I saw. "Kendall and I have never and will never be together. She is my best friend and will always be in my life. You can choose right now what you want to do because I'm going to choose her every time."

She sat for a moment then nodded her head.

"I will find my way back to campus." She gathered her purse as she spoke. "I refuse to be with any man who does not put me first. You have expressed where you stand, and I have no choice but to respect that. But I will never be a number two."

I nodded my head in understanding. We might not be on the same page as far as our relationship, but she was out of her mind if she thought that I was going to let her "find her way" anywhere.

"I completely understand where you stand, and I respect that as well, but where the hell do you think you are going?"

She looked back at me, confused, half out the car.

"I'm sorry, did I miss something? Did we not just break up?"

"Yeah, but that doesn't mean I'm going to change who I am. What do I look like, letting you roam around here, looking like a lost puppy?" She laughed a little. "If you want to go home, I will take you. If not, I will take you wherever you want to go. But I can't have it on my conscience that I just left you stranded."

She rolled her eyes as she got back in the car. We sat in silence for a moment before she started talking.

"I do not want us to break up, Aaron."

"I don't either," I spoke truthfully.

I believe I really liked her because she knew exactly who she was and who she was going to be. There was never any guessing for her. She had her life planned out and calculated. She would go to school for computer science with a concentration in application developer and, as soon as she gets out, land a job at a high-tech web-browser company, get married, and have three kids—in that order, no deviation. While she had all that planned out, I had yet to declare a major. Even Kendall, who was always all over the place when it came to making a decision, had decided she wanted to go into advertisement. She wanted her name to be on anything a man woman or child could look at. I believe that Melanie brought structure into my life, which I so desperately needed.

"Can we make a compromise?" she asked.

"What would that be?"

"I'm not going to ask you to stop talking to or being friends with her. All I ask is that when we are together, I am number one."

She finished her proposal, and I was the one sitting in silence. I thought back to all the girls that I dated, and Melanie was the only one I liked as much as Sasha. I thought back to all the times Kendall would need something or just want to talk, and I would drop everything to make sure she was good. I loved Kendall, but I knew that, if I could not be with her, I was never going to be in a healthy relationship, not if I jumped to her beck and call.

"I think that is something I can work out."

Aaron
2015

I throw the diary across the room and scream, "Fuck."

It hits her Nelly poster and slams to the floor as I pace the room, trying to figure out my next move. Kendall rushes back in the room.

"Aaron. I'm sorry. That had nothing to do with you," she pleaded, referring to her episode, but I cannot answer.

I still see red. I go over to where the diary landed and bring it back to her.

"Who the fuck is he?" She stares at the diary, not saying anything. "Kendall, answer the damn question," I scream.

I cannot control my anger. I have been through a lot in my thirty-one years of life, had my share of disappointments, my sprawls with the unwitting, even got arrested a time or two, but there has never been a time that I have experienced anger as I am now. I throw the diary past her head, and it hits the wall by the door. She is still standing staring, frozen.

"Kendall, damnit, answer me," I plead, almost in tears.

She has the same look as before—glassed-over eyes and spaced-out stare.

"I'm sorry," she whispers over and over.

I look at her, feeling defeated.

"Kendall, I'm sorry. Please talk to me. Tell me who did that to you," I soften my voice, trying to get her to snap out of the trance that she is in.

I pull her in to a hug as I look at the door, noticing that Kendall had not closed it all the way. Ms. Cynthia is standing in the doorway, with Ty standing behind her. As I hold Kendall, I can no longer hold in my tears.

"She won't tell me who did it," I cry.

Ms. Cynthia and Ty comes into the room, closing the door behind them. Ty stands against the door as Ms. Cynthia pries Kendall out of my arms. I fall back into the desk, sobbing into my hands.

"Remember your breathing," Ms. Cynthia says, taking Kendall to sit on the bed. "Come on, breathe with me."

I can hear them breathing through my cry.

"Levi," Ty's voice halts their breathing session.

It feels instant how my anguish turns back into rage. I look up from my hands. Kendall is staring at the ground as Ms. Cynthia stares at Ty.

"Tyson Phillips, what exactly are you accusing my son of?" Ms. Cynthia asks through clenched teeth.

I look from Ty to Kendall, realizing that she is back in reality. She is staring at the floor, shaking her leg. Kendall has always had a tell when she is caught. She will do one of two things: either fiddle with her hair or shake her left leg. Never the right. It is always the left. The same way she is doing right now.

I get off the desk and head for the door.

"Move," I demand, but Ty does not budge.

"He's not worth it. He's not worth going to prison for."

"Ty, move," I demand a second time.

"If you want to fight somebody, fight me." He clenches his jaw as he talks.

Growing up, people always thought that we were brothers instead of cousins. He and I are the same age, but he looks to be at least two years younger. He and I had always been about the same height. In recent years I've been more in the gym, so I have grown more muscular.

"Now, why would I want to fight you, Tyson?" I ask through my teeth.

"Because I didn't tell anybody that I suspected something in the tenth grade. I didn't know what, but I knew something was off. To be honest, I still don't know, but I figured whatever it is—he did it."

I step back a moment and look at him holding back tears.

"It's something bad, isn't it?" He tried to hold it all in.

"How dare you come in here and accuse my son of something you don't know anything about," Ms. Cynthia snaps at Ty.

I look at Kendall, who was now shaking her leg faster. I go and kneel in front of her, stopping her leg from shaking and making it so she is looking at me.

"Hey." I force myself to smile at her. Her leg has stopped, but she instantly starts playing with a piece of hair that had fallen out of her ponytail. I take both her hands and hold them in mine as I talk, "Ken. Right now, it's just me and you. Just us talking like old times. Remember laying on the roof and staring at the stars all night only for you to never find the Big Dipper." She smirks a bit as she looks at me then toward her mom and Ty.

"Hey. Look at me." She brings her attention back to me, and I caress her face. "Just me and you, Kendog, til the wheels fall off." She rolls her eyes and smirks again.

"I really do miss you," she says. Tears fall as I wipe them away.

"I know. I'm the best, right."

She chuckles and responds, "To say the least." I give her a genuine, halfhearted smile until she let out a deep breath before saying the words I needed to hear. "It was Levi."

My face turns cold as I stand and go back toward the door. Ty is still standing in the same place.

"I don't believe you," Ms. Cynthia yells.

I see Kendall getting up from the bed in her dismay.

"Move," I say to Ty, who once again does not budge.

"Are you serious?" Kendall questions.

"Move," I almost holler.

"It's not worth it."

My frustration and anger take over as I pick up the diary from the floor. The page I read was easy to find because of the pages.

"You read this and tell me it's not worth it."

Tenth Grade, 2000
Kendall
Age Sixteen

"Levi is taking you! That is the end of this discussion."

I followed my dad as he moved through the house, getting ready for work.

"I'm not protesting a chaperone. Aaron can take me."

He shook his head in disagreement and said, "Aaron has a game, and you cannot count on Aaron for everything you need. Your brother is more than capable, and he wants to go to the movies anyway. Two birds."

He shrugged and turned to walk past me.

"Then I'm not going. I will just call Micah and cancel." He stopped moving around me and finally looked at me. "Levi will just mess everything up, and I will not have fun. Isn't that the whole purpose of a first date?" I pleaded my case.

"I have already talked to Micah's parents, so you're going. And you are going to have a great time. Don't let your brother ruin your day. Just ignore him." He pulled me into a hug.

"That's easier said than done," I mumbled.

Levi sat on the couch as I came into the living room. My dad had just gotten home. He sat across from Levi in his favorite reclining chair. I picked my outfit specifically knowing that Levi was taking me, and I had to be ready for anything. I wore some Baby Phat blue jeans with a white shirt that slightly showed my midriff. It had a gold Baby Phat logo in the center. I made sure to wear tennis shoes, white Reeboks, just in case I need to run. Levi licked his lips as I came in. I pretended not to notice.

"You look great, sweetie," Daddy said, sitting up in his chair, noticing my entrance.

"Where is Momma?"

Dad got up to get his camera out of his desk drawer.

"She had a house showing tonight and couldn't make it." I rolled my eyes, knowing that she was not at a showing at six o'clock at night. "Come on and smile, baby girl. It's my Ken-doll's first date. Look excited."

I put my hand on my hip and conjured up the fakest smile I could. Levi chuckled behind my dad, making me even more uncomfortable.

"Okay, Pop, we need to go before the two lovebirds miss the movie," Levi announced anxiously.

My dad took his picture and stared at me.

"Now who told you that you could grow up on me, Doll?" he asked, pulling me into a hug.

I smiled as I sucked in his scent, saying, "You did, Daddy."

He laughed his hardy laugh.

"Well, I suppose I did." He kissed my forehead. "You have a good time, and call me if you need anything at all."

He kissed me again before letting me go.

When I walked out the house, Levi was already in my dad's maroon 1996 Buick Regal. I went to the passenger-side back door and tried to get in, but the door was locked. I rolled my eyes as he rolled down the passenger-side front window.

"Hop up front. You can get in the back when what's his face gets in."

"Lord, please let this be a good night," I prayed before opening the front passenger door and getting in.

The ride to Micah's house was quiet other than the radio blasting. We were halfway there when Levi started talking.

"You look nice."

"Thanks," I plainly spoke as I looked out the window.

"So what's up with this Micah guy? You really like him?"

I looked at him, confused on how to answer the question. If I did not like him, I would not be going on a date with him, but I could not tell Levi that I really liked anybody.

"He's okay," I said, deciding that that would be a safe answer.

"Just okay? The guy that takes my sister on her first date has to be more than just okay."

Again, I am confused on how to reply. Luckily, we had reached Micah's house before I had to give an answer. Micah and I rode in the backseat on the way to the movies. Every now and then I would see Levi staring at me in the rearview mirror. It made the ride more awkward and stressful.

We finally made it to the movies, and thankfully, Levi was not going in the same movie that we were. We decided to see *Love & Basketball,* and he saw *28 Days Later.* We sat in the center of the theater—the best seats in my opinion. Halfway through the movie, I loosened up, and he put his arm around me and pulled me closer to him. I had to use the restroom since the movie started, but I tried my best to hold it. A little while after he put his arm around me, I could not hold it anymore.

"I have to pee," I whispered. He chuckled before moving his arm. "Let me know what happens," I said before getting up.

I went to the restroom, smiling. I was happy because the date was going well so far. Micah and I were getting along, and Levi was not there, making it weird.

I checked myself out in the mirror before leaving the restroom. I smiled at myself, acknowledging that I still looked good. I walked out and was immediately snatched into a corner.

"So you going to just let him be all over you like that?" Levi said in my face.

I tried to turn my face away from him.

"I don't know what you are talking about."

I tried to hold my composure.

"I see you all under him. He's just okay, huh?" He puts his hand on my stomach. "Does he touch you like this?"

"Levi, please," I whispered. I can see people noticing us. "People are staring."

He scuffed before removing his hand.

"We'll talk later," he said before leaving me.

I saw Ty looking at me, confused. I didn't want to answer any questions. I knew that if he was there, that meant the game was over, and more than likely, Aaron was there too. I went back in the restroom, into a stall, and broke down.

"Hey, are you okay?" I heard from the stall next to mine.

"Yeah, sorry," I managed.

"He's not worth the tears, girl," she said.

"Huh?" I questioned, confused.

"I assume it's about a boy. Don't give him the satisfaction of your tears."

"Thank you," I said as I heard the stall door open and close.

I got myself together as much as I could before returning to the movie, which was almost over.

"I was starting to get concerned. You were gone for so long," Micah whispered in my ear.

"I'm good. Do you think your mom can pick us up? I think my brother left."

He looked at me, confused.

"I will check when the movie lets out."

Kendall
2015

Anger musters as my mother talks.

"I raised my son to be a respectable man."

"You raised your son to be a molester and a rapist," I argue, meeting my mother in the center of the room. "You want to know when it started, Mom? It started right after you and Daddy got divorced. You want to know how long it lasted? Until the eleventh grade. I'm not sure if you can count or not, but that is eleven years." She shakes her head, breaking our standoff and going to sit at the desk. I follow behind, "All of those nights you would leave him to 'babysit.'"

The memories send chills down my body. When I had to go to the hospital, my senior year in college was the first time I had an episode. After I left the hospital, they became more frequent, especially when Levi came back from Florida. Just the thought of him touching me would have been enough to send me into an episode. After leaving the hospital, I had to do mandatory therapy sessions twice a week, one alone and one with my parents so they would know how to handle my episodes. At the start of the sessions Levi asked to join, but the rules were parents or guardians only. It was about our third or fourth session of just me and Lydia, my therapist, when I told her everything. She made me repeat that it was not my fault until I actually believed it. Now days having one is very rare. The two

I had today I believe were from the stress and being back here at my dad's.

I am not at all surprised at my mother's reaction to everything being in the open. My whole life Levi was her golden child. He could do no wrong. When she and my dad divorced, they gave us a choice of who we wanted to stay with the majority of our time. At that time, Levi had not touched me. He was a little distant when we all lived together. I figured it was because I am a girl, and maybe he just did not like playing with girls. Levi decided that he wanted to stay with my mother, and I chose my dad. I am not sure if that triggered something in him, but the first night I stayed at my mother's was when everything started. After the second time, I tried to tell my mother, but she brushed it off and said that he was just rough playing and would make sure that he did not "play so rough." After the first couple of times of me trying to tell my mother, Levi would always "punish" me. I even tried to tell my dad once. That was one of the worse times. I could hardly walk. He was very strategic as to make it so there were no marks or bruises.

"I wonder how many other poor girls he has done this to."

"Aaron, no!"

I hear a scream from downstairs. I hear a crash and people hollering from the front yard. I had not realized that Ty and Aaron left the room. I join my mother at the window as we watch Aaron and Ty attack Levi with no mercy.

"They are going to kill him," my mother screams as she opens the window. "Somebody help him. Get them off him."

Some people looked up at the window, some watched in awe, but two of my cousins tried to pull them off him.

As I watch, it seems like everything is going in slow motion. It is like for every time they strike him, it is in direct correlation with every touch. The blood gushing from his mouth is for every tear I cried. For so long I wondered what would happen if everything came out in the open. I wondered how I would feel. As I stand here, I feel nothing. I thought there might be some joy in seeing Aaron go at him. Hell, I might even cheer him on, "Kick his ass." But there is nothing. I look at my mother who is sitting on the window bench, crying.

"Why do you try to protect him? Since I can remember, you've always taken up for him. Why?"

She looks up at me, makeup smeared.

"The world is so hard on our men. At least my son always has his mother to fall back on."

I frown at her.

"And what about your daughter?" I almost holler.

"You had your father."

I chuckle and shake my head, moving away from her.

"A child needs a father and a mother. You cannot pick which child you want to protect."

She looks back to the window and screams, "Oh my god!"

She gets up and runs out the room. I go back to the window and see Levi lying on the ground, barely moving. He is on his back, and I can see him trying to focus. As I close the window, I see that he has focused on the window. I close it and move away.

I sit on my bed, trying to collect my thoughts.

"Hey," I hear Sasha at the door.

"You okay?" she asks as she comes in the room, closing the door.

"I think I will be."

I smile slightly as she sits on the bed beside me, pulling me into a side hug. She looks around the bed for a moment then gives me a side eye.

"When I left earlier, the bed did not look like this. I know because I sat on it." She realizes what she is saying and jumps up from the bed. "Ew, did you two…"

I chuckle.

"Huh?" I question as if I did not hear her.

"I will just sit over here at the desk… Unless that isn't safe either. How about you just tell me where to sit."

I laugh as she tries to figure things out.

"The desk is fine."

She shakes her head.

"Y'all nasty," she says as she sits. "Before you go back home, cheap wine and cheesy movies are in order."

I nod and agree, "I'm always up for a little winecheesy."

"And you will tell me what the hell just happened."

I sigh and said, "That is going to take something a lot stronger than wine."

"Whatever you need. Just let me know."

I nod.

"Ty and Aaron left."

"Do you have Aaron's number?" I ask.

She smiles as she stands.

"It's the same number it's always been."

I smile back and nod.

She comes over to me and said, "We are about to go. I will call you later to check on you."

I get up and give her a hug.

"Tell my babies I will see them later."

She pulls away.

"Sure will. Love you, girl."

"Love you."

She leaves as I sit back on the bed, getting my phone from the nightstand. I go to my contacts, and Aaron's name is the first to come up. I hit call, and he answers on the first ring.

"I'm not sorry."

"I didn't ask you to be. Are you okay?"

"I think I broke my hand." He laughs. "Ty says he's sorry for not saying anything sooner. He is beating himself up about it."

I sigh. Ty came up to me at school after I saw him at the movies on my first date. He asked what was going on, and I brushed it off and asked him to leave it alone.

"Is he with you?"

"Yeah. You want to talk to him?"

"Yeah."

I wait for Ty to get on the phone, and I feel bad. The last thing I want is for either one of them to feel bad about any of this. I know now that it was not my fault, but in some ways, it still feels like it was.

"Yeah," he answers the phone, clearly upset.

"I owe you an apology. I should have told you everything a long time ago, but I was scared. I don't want you feeling bad for my fears."

He is quiet for a moment then responds, "Kendall, you are and have always been a sister to me. I knew something wasn't right, and I didn't say anything. What happened past that day is on me, and I can't forgive myself."

I drop my head, listening to him.

"Ty."

"Naw, Ken. You were a victim. You cannot blame yourself. It was our job to take care of you. Trust it won't happen again."

I hear the phone rustle then Aaron's voice, "Hey."

I lay back in the bed.

"Hey."

I feel a slight smile creep on my face. Since Aaron and I stopped talking, I had to find a different form of normalcy that never felt normal. Talking to him made me realize how much I need him in my life. The only issue is I know that we cannot be.

The thought of losing him again feels so much worse than the first time because this time it will simply be because we cannot be together.

"Thank you for coming today. I think we both needed it."

"Yeah, we did," he agrees.

There is a pause.

"Thank you for handling Levi," I say, relieved that it is all in the open.

"If he even breathes your way, you call me or Ty. Even when you go back home. He needs to know that he is not safe anywhere. If I could have killed him, I would have, but somebody said that the police were on the way."

"I'm glad you left in time."

There is another pause, then my mother opens the door.

"I'm taking Levi to the hospital and try to talk him out of pressing charges. I assume you are talking to Aaron."

I look at her without answering.

"Well, tell him I said thank you for letting him live," I scuff. "It won't happen a second time," I answer for Aaron.

"I will be back tomorrow."

I shake my head.

"Don't bother. I'm going back home tomorrow night," I lie.

She nods before closing the door again.

"Next time I see him, it's a body bag," Aaron says through his teeth.

"Well, it won't be anytime soon," I say in an attempt to calm him down.

"Are you really leaving tomorrow?"

"No."

He sighs this time.

"Do you think maybe we can…"

"No," I say, plainly cutting him off before letting him finish. "The next time I see you, I want you." He does not say anything. "Aaron, I love you, but…"

He cut me off this time, "I know. Just know if you ever need anything at all, my number will never change." I sigh.

"I don't want this to be the last time we talk."

I struggle with myself. I know that he and I cannot be what we were, or even talk the way we did. But I have never wanted something more in my entire life. It is a struggle between what I want and what I know is good for the both of us in our current situation. I do not know what he and Melanie's relationship is like, but there is a child involved, and that complicates everything even more.

"Neither do I, but we both know that we will never be just friends again. I want you, but I'm with her."

I sit up in the bed.

"So leave her," I almost yell.

"I wish it was that easy. I'm pulling up to Ty's place now."

I take a deep breath and say, "From now on, the ball is in your court. When you are ready, I am here. No more avoiding you."

He and I share a slight laugh.

"I'm happy to hear that."

"Okay, let me get off this phone before I change my mind and tell you to come back later." There is another pause as I contemplate the invitation. "I love you, Aaron. Always will."

"And I love you, more than you know. Talk to you soon."

He hangs up, and I stare at the phone. I smile and place the phone back on the nightstand. I stand up and look around my room again. I really need to get rid of some of these shoes. I notice the plate of food still sitting on the desk. I chuckle before going to get it. I grab the plate and take one more glance at the room before leaving, closing the door behind me.

National Sexual Assault Hotline
(800.656.HOPE and online.rainn.org)